The Decade of the 2000s

Science and Technology of the 2000s

Other titles in *The Decade of the 2000s* series:

The Decade of the 2000s

Science and Technology of the 2000s

By Harry Henderson

ReferencePoint Press®

San Diego, CA

© 2014 ReferencePoint Press, Inc.
Printed in the United States

For more information, contact:
ReferencePoint Press, Inc.
PO Box 27779
San Diego, CA 92198
www.ReferencePointPress.com

LIBRARY OF CONGRESS CATALOGING-IN-PUBLICATION DATA

Henderson, Harry, 1951–
  Science and technology of the 2000s / by Harry Henderson.
    pages cm. -- (The decade of the 2000s)
  Audience: Grade 9 to 12.
  Includes bibliographical references and index.
  ISBN -13: 978-1-60152-528-4 (hardback)
  ISBN-10: 1-60152-528-1 (hardback)
  1. Science--History--21st century--Juvenile literature. 2. Technology--History--21st century--Juvenile literature. I. Title.
  Q126.4.H459 2014
  500--dc23
                                                                        2013018907

Contents

2002
- Euro enters circulation
- Terrorists attack Bali tourist district in Indonesia
- Dwarf planet Quaoar is discovered
- *American Idol* debuts on Fox network
- Xbox Live revolutionizes online gaming

2004
- Hundreds of thousands die in Indian Ocean tsunami
- *Spirit* and *Opportunity* rovers explore surface of Mars
- Facebook is launched
- Hundreds die when Chechen separatists take over a school in Russia
- Palestinian leader Yasser Arafat dies
- Green Belt Movement founder Wangari Maathai of Kenya wins Nobel Peace Prize

2000
- Dire warnings of Y2K Millennium Bug fizzle
- Dot-com bubble bursts
- Israel withdraws all forces from Lebanon
- Dashboard GPS devices become widely available
- Tiger Woods becomes youngest golfer to win Grand Slam
- USS *Cole* is attacked in Yemen

2000   2001   2002   2003   2004

2001
- Terrorist attack on United States kills three thousand people
- Apple launches iPod
- World's first space tourist reaches International Space Station
- Film version of first Harry Potter book is released
- Wikipedia is launched
- United States invades Afghanistan
- Netherlands legalizes same-sex marriage

2003
- United States invades Iraq
- Space shuttle *Columbia* disintegrates on reentry
- Human genome project is completed
- Record heat wave kills tens of thousands in Europe
- China launches its first manned space mission
- WHO issues rare global health alert on SARS

2005
- YouTube is launched
- Burst levees flood New Orleans during Hurricane Katrina
- Kyoto Protocol on climate change goes into effect
- National Academies releases human embryonic stem cell research guidelines
- Earthquake devastates Kashmir
- Lance Armstrong wins seventh consecutive Tour de France (later stripped of all titles)

2008
- United States elects Barack Obama, first African American president
- Oil prices hit record high of $147 per barrel
- US Olympic swimmer Michael Phelps wins record eight gold medals
- Islamic militants attack financial district in Mumbai, India
- Universal Declaration of Human Rights marks sixtieth anniversary

2005   2006   2007   2008   2009

2006
- Pluto is demoted to dwarf planet status
- North Korea conducts its first nuclear test
- Saddam Hussein is executed in Iraq
- West African black rhino is declared extinct
- Twitter is launched
- Global warming documentary, *An Inconvenient Truth,* is released

2009
- WHO declares swine flu outbreak an international pandemic
- Mouse genome is fully sequenced
- Michael Jackson dies at his home in California
- World's tallest man-made structure is completed in Dubai
- Large Hadron Collider becomes world's highest-energy particle accelerator
- Widespread match-fixing scandal rocks European soccer

2007
- Mitchell report details rampant PED use in baseball
- Apple debuts iPhone
- Dozens killed and wounded in mass shooting at Virginia Tech
- Arctic sea ice hits record low
- Google Street View is launched
- Prime Minister Benazir Bhutto of Pakistan is assassinated
- Amazon releases its Kindle
- Great Recession, worldwide economic crisis, begins

Expectations and Surprises

Science and technology in the first decade of the twenty-first century brought their share of surprises (both good and bad), new capabilities, and ongoing concerns. Computer users, particularly in governments and large corporations, breathed a collective sigh of relief when the morning of January 1, 2000, rolled around and the feared Y2K bug failed to wreak havoc. In a few cases the year 2000 was mistakenly read by software as 1900, but by and large the effort to find and fix faulty date code in millions of lines of aging computer programs had succeeded. All that remained were lingering questions over whether the $134 billion cost (in the United States alone) of fixes had been justified.

The Web Comes of Age

During the decade the World Wide Web continued to expand rapidly. In 2000 about 350 million people were online, but by 2010 that number had swelled to nearly 2 billion. The user base had also spread out, with the fastest growth in Asia, followed by Europe and North America. But while many people continued to have faith in the power of the web, the decade started off with the bursting of a dot-com bubble of overhyped Internet businesses that greatly contributed to a stock market crash that wiped out about $5 trillion in market value.

However, the web proved to be resilient, and its power to connect people to information (and to each other) only grew. Google founders Larry Page and Sergey Brin, soon joined by CEO Eric Schmidt, turned a clever search engine into an indispensable tool—so much so, that *google* became a commonly used verb. Apple CEO Steve Jobs rescued a faltering computer company and reinvented it as a mobile media giant. Apple's talented designers and engineers first put music in peoples' pockets with iPods, then married media, software, and GPS to create the iPhone—probably the most lusted-after gadget of the decade.

Access to information and the power of mobile devices were joined by a social revolution. By 2009 Facebook alone had more users than the whole web had back in 2000. Blogs, or online diaries, became popular by mid-decade not only for individual expression, but as a tool for new forms of journalism and political activism. Just as blogs seemed to be peaking in 2006, the first tweets of a new storm of online expression were being heard—by the end of the decade Twitter usage was approaching 50 million tweets a day.

A computer user sends a tweet to his Twitter followers. This new, more concise form of online expression took hold when Twitter launched in 2006.

Science Probes New Realms

Advances in science also marked the decade. Often these advances were possible because of the capabilities of new technology. The intrepid twin robotic Mars rovers *Spirit* and *Opportunity* explored the landscape of the Red Planet and confirmed the presence of life-supporting water. Humans continued to pursue ultimate questions—how we evolved here on Earth, who our ancestors were, and whether life and intelligence exist elsewhere in the universe. The discovery of hundreds of planets circling distant suns brought the first hints of Earth-like worlds, but no definite answers.

Here on Earth scientists built the huge Large Hadron Collider, preparing to launch a search for the Higgs boson, so-called God particle that could explain the nature of mass itself. Other researchers looked for dark matter and the even more mysterious dark energy—strange substances that together apparently make up about 95 percent of the universe. Science also met engineering through nanotechnology, offering the ability to build virtually anything "from the atoms up." Other researchers pursued the continuing quest for ever faster computers—an endeavor that involved both quantum physics and biology. Meanwhile robots continued to roll (or walk) out of science fiction and into everyday life.

In biology and medical science the biggest news was the completion of the Human Genome Project and its spelling out of the instructions that specify the structure and function of the human body. New diagnostic tests became available. Gene replacement therapy and stem cell infusions began to offer some hope for treating some of the most difficult and destructive diseases, but there were tragic setbacks as well as modest successes.

The decade of the 2000s ended, as it had begun, with another economic bubble and a more severe recession even as new technologies such as tablet computers and ever-more capable smartphones continued to emerge. New services attracted excitement, but also concern as governments and corporations now seem to know not only who people are but where they are and what they are doing. Clearly, the century's surprises have just begun.

Chapter ONE

Cellular Secrets

Many futurists have suggested that if the twentieth century was the century of physics, the twenty-first century will be the century of biology. In June 2000 US president Bill Clinton and UK prime minister Tony Blair jointly announced that the entire human genome—the chemical instructions for life—had been transcribed in draft form.

The human genome was revealed to consist of about twenty thousand genes, each a sequence of chemical bases (adenine, cytosine, guanine, and thymine—referred to as A, C, G, T) that "spell out" all of the numerous proteins that make up every structure in the human body. By definition, each gene has an identifiable correspondence to some characteristic, trait, or process in the organism. Thus if A, C, G, T is the "alphabet," a gene is like a word, and the whole genome is like a vast dictionary.

By the end of the 2000s, researchers had advanced to the point that DNA sequences could be rearranged, edited, and written using something like the genetic equivalent of a word processor. At first, existing viruses were assembled from separate sequences, but a new world dawned in 2010 when biologist and entrepreneur J. Craig Venter announced the culmination of a fifteen-year-long, $40 million project. An entire genome for a bacterium called *Mycoplasma mycoides* had been built up from "raw" chemical components and transplanted into another bacterium whose own DNA had been removed. The result was, according to Venter, "the first self-replicating species . . . on the planet whose parent is a computer."[1]

Meanwhile, practical medical applications came slowly. However, throughout the 2000s researchers not only read the "sentences" spelled out by about twenty thousand human genes, they began to devise ways to correct the tragic errors that underlay devastating diseases. Unfortunately, there were missteps and setbacks along the way.

Another biological revolution of the 2000s involved stem cells, which began to be used to create skin and even to repair damaged hearts. However, this technology, too, caused controversy, especially because the stem cells were derived from human embryos.

Gene Therapy: Replacing Defective Genes

Jesse Gelsinger, seventeen, was born with a condition called OTC deficiency. It is a genetically caused disorder in which the body cannot properly produce an enzyme needed to break down ammonia, which accumulates, damaging organs and causing other problems. Babies with OTC usually die, but Gelsinger's version of the disease was less severe. He was able to manage it with a combination of a low-protein diet and thirty-two pills a day.

In 1998 Gelsinger learned of a University of Pennsylvania study that was testing a treatment that could replace the defective gene and greatly improve the body's ability to get rid of the toxic ammonia. Gelsinger wanted to help save babies from the disease—and perhaps if the treatment were successful, he would not have to stick to a special diet and take all those pills each day. Gelsinger was told the treatment was risky. Still, he told a friend, "What's the worse [sic] that can happen to me? I die, and it's for the babies."[2] Gelsinger's gene therapy used a weakened cold virus (adenovirus) to insert corrective genes into his liver. He was told that this method had been tried on mice, monkeys, baboons, and one earlier human patient, with no serious side effects.

For Gelsinger the results were tragically different. On September 13, 1999, he received the injection of gene-bearing virus. He became jaundiced (a sign of liver failure), his kidneys failed, and his blood could not clot properly. Finally, his lungs failed and he died on September 17. After his death, the US Food and Drug Administration investigated and concluded that the researchers had not followed proper procedures or provided full information about the risks of the treatment. Although the University of Pennsylvania denied wrongdoing, it paid an undisclosed sum of money to Gelsinger's parents. Researcher Leon Rosenberg, looking back on these events, said, "Those were terrible days. The field bottomed out. The integrity of science was damaged tremendously."[3]

Overcoming Challenges

The story of gene therapy thus began the 2000s with unanswered questions and numerous challenges. If safe genetic therapies could be developed, they would represent one of the biggest advances in medicine since vaccines and antibiotics. There are more than four thousand diseases that are directly caused by defective genes. Many of these diseases, such as the lung disease cystic fibrosis, are life-threatening or debilitating. A number of cancers, such as melanoma (a form of skin cancer), may also be susceptible to gene therapy.

Finding a safe way to get corrective genes into the body proved difficult. If a virus is used to carry genes to the targeted cells, the body can

Test tubes containing the entire human genome—that is, all of the DNA found in a human cell—are stored for future research in a laboratory refrigerator. The international effort to sequence the human genome was completed in 2003.

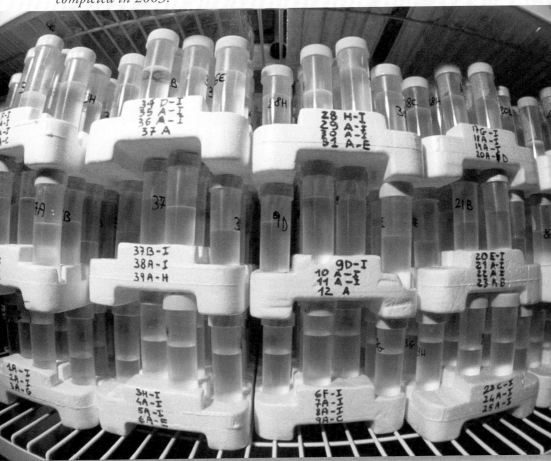

Choosing Baby's Genes?

Picture a woman whose parents suffer from Alzheimer's disease, a condition that may be caused by a gene defect. She goes to a geneticist, who extracts her eggs and examines them carefully to determine which eggs have copies of the gene that are free of the defect. Those eggs are fertilized and implanted into the woman's uterus. When her daughter is born, she will grow up having dodged at least one genetic bullet.

Such a procedure first happened in 2002. It was the work of prenatal genetics pioneer Yury Verlinsky. For families with a history of serious genetically based disease, such procedures can bring a great deal of relief from anxiety.

However, medical ethicists have sounded a cautionary note. It is one thing to be able to ensure one's child is free of disease. Some fear that people who can afford these rather expensive procedures might use them to produce offspring with specific traits or enhancements. Marian Damewood, director of women's and children's services at York Hospital in Pennsylvania, worries that if these techniques are perfected, "we'd be getting very close to designing a human being who's going to have no flaws and live forever."

Would normally produced human beings with their random assortment of good and bad genes come to be treated as second-class citizens, unable to compete? It may be decades before geneticists know enough to ensure superior intelligence, agility, or appearance. Perhaps that will be long enough for a new ethics to emerge to guide such decisions.

Quoted in Infei Chen, "Dodging Alzheimer's with Clever Genetics," *Discover*, January 2003, p. 37.

react in several ways. Tissue attacked by the virus can become inflamed. The body's immune system, designed precisely to detect and kill invading viruses, could respond violently, perhaps killing the virus before it can do its job. Worse still, the genes carried by the virus could trigger oncogenes (cancer genes) in the body.

One condition researchers hoped to target with gene therapy is called severe combined immune deficiency, or "bubble baby syndrome." Children with this genetic condition essentially have no defense against germs and must be kept sealed away from contact with people and the outside world. Previously, the only effective treatment was a bone marrow transplant, a difficult procedure even when a donor can be found. However, if the defective gene could be replaced, the body would start producing normal immune system cells.

Genetic treatments in 2000 were successful in restoring the immune systems of ten patients, but even this success soon revealed a dark side. During the next few years, four of the patients developed leukemia, a type of blood cancer. Investigators think that the virus used to carry the repair gene accidentally activated a cancer gene. Researchers hoped to avoid this result in the future by modifying the virus and their method of insertion.

Restoring Sight?

At a time when most kids were exploring the world with increasing confidence and learning to read, seven-year-old Corey Haas was going blind. Corey suffered from Leber's congenital amaurosis, an inherited retinal disease for which there was no treatment. However, the pioneering research of geneticist and doctor Jean Bennett and her husband, retinal surgeon Albert Maguire, led in the development of an experimental gene replacement procedure in 2008.

Eye diseases offered one of the better targets for gene therapy. The eye has relatively few cells, and they are confined to a small area, which makes it easier to target them without risking a "spillover" to other cells. Also, the eye is not guarded as vigorously by the immune system, reducing the chance of an immune reaction.

Corey received an injection in his left eye just after his eighth birthday. A swarm of viruses carried the replacement genes to his retinal cells. As writer Pam Belluck reported in 2009, "Now 9, Corey plays Little League baseball, drives go-carts, navigates wooded trails near his home in Hadly, N.Y. and reads the blackboard in class. 'It's gotten, like, really, better,' he said."[4]

Corey was part of a study involving five children and seven adults from Belgium, Italy, and the United States. As Stephen Rose, whose Foundation Fighting Blindness helped pay for the study, summarized, "All 12 had significant improvement. You're not returning 20-20 vision, let's be real, but you're returning a tremendous amount of vision."[5]

The Promise of Stem Cells

Human embryonic stem cells were discovered by James Thomson at the University of Wisconsin in 1998. These are the cells that, in a complex process that is far from fully understood, eventually become all the organs, bones, muscles, and tissues of the human body. What makes embryonic stem cells particularly valuable, however, is that they retain pluripotency—the ability to turn into almost any specific kind of cell when placed in the correct environment.

Embryonic stem cells offered researchers the opportunity to learn much more about how the many different types of cells in the body develop. However, embryonic cells proved to be very hard to manipulate and control. For example, unless very precise conditions are maintained, embryonic cells will rapidly differentiate into unwanted forms, including cancer cells. Because of these difficulties, there were no clinical studies using embryonic stem cells in humans during the decade.

Another obstacle to the use of embryonic stem cells involved beliefs about human life itself. Embryonic stem cells come from the very early embryo, known as a blastocyst. At this stage of development, the embryo is a minute clump of cells that have just begun to multiply and differentiate. For people who believe that human life is entitled to protection from the moment of conception, the destruction of an embryo in order to provide stem cells is unacceptable.

In 2001 President George W. Bush issued an order banning federal funding of research using embryonic stem cells, except certain existing cell lines that had already been grown. Although privately funded research could still be carried out, embryonic stem cell research in the United States was limited for most of the decade. In 2006 Congress twice passed legislation that would allow stem cells to be harvested from embryos that had been frozen and stored by fertility clinics. Bush vetoed the legislation both times.

The 2008 election of President Barack Obama changed the political landscape. In March 2009 the president issued an executive order that removed most of the Bush-era restrictions and increased federal funding for research on embryonic stem cells. More stem cells lines were approved for use.

New Sources of Stem Cells

Researchers also found an alternative to using the controversial embryonic stem cells. It turned out that stem cells could be found in the body

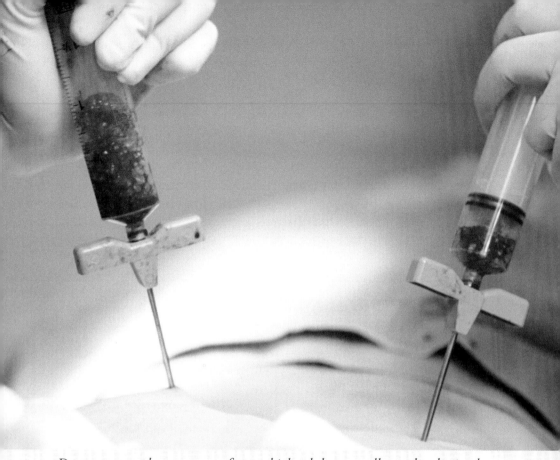

Doctors extract bone marrow from which adult stem cells can be obtained. Embryonic stem cells have potentially greater benefits than adult stem cells, but they are controversial. In 2007 researchers demonstrated a new method for creating stem cells with all of the flexibility of embryonic stem cells but none of the controversy.

even after a person is born. These so-called adult or somatic stem cells are particularly abundant in the bone marrow. Since no embryos need to be destroyed to obtain these cells, their use is much less controversial. Further, the possibility of using stem cells from a patient's own bone marrow would avoid rejection by the immune system.

In 2007 researchers at Kyoto University in Japan and at the University of Wisconsin–Madison demonstrated that ordinary human skin cells could be reprogrammed through genetic and chemical manipulation to turn into stem cells. Called induced pluripotent stem cells, these might have the same advantages as bone marrow stem cells and also be easier to obtain. There remained the risk that genetic programming errors could create cancer cells, but later researchers found a way to create stem cells using only chemical processes, thus entirely eliminating that risk.

Thus, rather than using the troublesome embryonic stem cells, researchers seeking new medical treatments turned to stem cells from patients' own bodies. As the decade continued, numerous experimental studies seemed to suggest that stem cells could be used effectively to treat a variety of conditions. In 2000 French researchers used stem cells from the thighs of their patients to try to improve their heart function. Although the doctors observed some improvement, many of the patients developed irregular heartbeats. The stem cells had grown into thigh muscles, which apparently did not work quite the same way as heart muscles.

How Should Genetic Tests Be Used?

By the end of the 2000s, the cost of genome analysis had fallen to a price many people could afford. There were even plans to offer some genetic tests over the counter at local drug stores. In 2007 Huntington Willard, director of the Duke Institute for Genome Science and Policy, observed, "Patients are receiving genomic tests and benefiting from them; there are real live people being taken care of now."

However, other experts say this does not necessarily mean that everyone should plan on getting their personal genome analyzed. Bioethcist Hank Greely warns that making appropriate decisions based on test results would be difficult for people without specialized knowledge. He says, "If people can order genetic information through the Web and get results without any health professional being involved, they might act on that information in harmful ways—either because they think they're safer than they actually are, or they think they're at greater risk than they actually are." For example, Greely notes, a woman whose test shows a low risk for breast cancer might decide she no longer needs to have regular mammograms.

In general, people are not very good at assessing health risks. Suppose a gene test shows a person has a 25 percent higher-than-normal risk of getting a disease. It may be, however, that this particular disease is very rare to begin with. The added risk therefore may not justify taking drastic preventative measures.

Quoted in Erika Check Hayden, "The Genome Turns Personal," *Discover*, January 2008, pp. 30–31.

Quoted in Robert Keating, "Interview: Bioethicist Hank Greely Speaks Out on the Vast Benefits and Troubling Risks of Sequencing Personal Genomes for Pennies on the Gene," *Discover*, January 2011, p. 60.

Rebuilding the Body

In 2005 Ruth Pavelko lay in an operating theater, surrounded by screens, scanners, and other high-tech equipment. She had pretty much run out of options. She had diabetes and had also suffered four heart attacks. Her clogged arteries were being held open with thirteen stents, but her heart was swollen and failing, struggling to keep pumping. Its numerous scars and dead muscle tissue showed clearly on the monitors. Using sophisticated 3-D mapping techniques and sensors, the doctors determined which of Pavelko's heart muscles were still contracting normally. Those would be the starting points in an attempt to repair her heart—not with some implanted device, but with the patient's own stem cells, harvested from her bone marrow.

For several months after the operation, Pavelko did not seem to notice any improvement. One day, however, she decided to wash some dishes. After she was finished, she realized that she had not had to stop to catch her breath and rest. Later she found she could do many of the other little, necessary things that had been difficult or impossible for her for six years.

Although stem cells from bone marrow had helped Pavelko, even better results might be expected using heart cells themselves. In 2009 doctors at the Cedars-Sinai Heart Institute in Los Angeles for the first time grew specialized stem cells from a patient's own heart tissue, and then injected them back into the heart. Heart institute director Eduardo Marbán noted, "Five years ago, we didn't even know the heart had its own distinct type of stem cells. Now we are exploring how to harness such stem cells to help patients heal their own damaged hearts."[6]

Growing Replacement Organs

Regenerative medicine that could grow replacement organs or bones as needed has long been a dream. During the 2000s tissue engineers used stem cells to grow skin, cartilage, and bone. The stem cells are placed on a plastic mold shaped like the desired structure, provided with nutrients, and allowed to grow. More complex structures such as a heart valve are more challenging. As a kind of shortcut, researchers have taken heart valves from donor cadavers, stripped them of their actual cells (which would provoke an immune reaction in the recipient), and used the remaining structure of elastin and collagen as the matrix for growing stem cells. By 2005 such hybrid valves had been shown to function well.

By the end of the decade, news of such successful uses of stem cells seemed to offer hope to desperate patients with failing hearts or severe spinal cord injuries. Numerous clinics in Mexico, China, and other countries had sprung up during this same period; many of these claimed to offer stem cell treatments for everything from blindness to Parkinson's to Alzheimer's disease. George Daley of the Harvard Stem Cell Institute noted, "There are patients being given spinal injections of cells for anything from cerebral palsy to Alzheimer's, and for many conditions there is absolutely no scientific evidence that this works."[7]

The Man with the Bionic Arm

The audience in the auditorium watched Jesse Sullivan intently as he picked up a glass of water, drank from it, and gently put it down. What made this so extraordinary was that Sullivan, an electrician, had to have both of his arms amputated in May 2001, after he accidentally touched a wire carrying 7,000 volts of electricity. But only seven weeks later, he had a new, robotic arm and hand that contained six motors and were controlled by a built-in computer.

Built by a team at the Rehabilitation Institute of Chicago, the arm receives its instructions not mechanically, but from Sullivan's brain and the nerve signals it sends. Four nerves that used to run to his arm were surgically rerouted to muscles in his chest. Now, when Sullivan thinks about what he wants to do with his arm, the nerve signals sent by his brain activate the chest muscles. These muscles in turn generate electrical signals that are picked up by electrodes in the chest and sent to the mechanical arm. A computer in the arm then interprets the signals and performs the desired movements.

Unlike earlier artificial arms that could pick up only one type of movement signal at a time, the new arm and hand can perform several types of movements at once, such as extending, turning, or grasping. Using the new arm, it is much easier for Sullivan to perform daily activities such as putting on his socks, shaving, or eating his breakfast. His robotic arm also has feedback. "I actually feel my hand open and close. It feels sort of like squeezing a tennis ball,"[8] he says.

Virtual Brains

As researchers during the 2000s learned more about the brain and how it communicates with the rest of the body, the first steps were being taken toward an even more ambitious goal: building something that works like a living brain. Since digital computers first appeared in the late 1940s, people have compared them to human brains. Computers can now do many things brains can—and indeed, can do many things (such as play chess) better than people can.

Actually, today's computers, although very powerful, do not work like brains do. Computers process data in orderly sequences and store or retrieve specific items from particular memory locations. They get much of their power from their sheer speed, processing billions of operations

A double amputee, wearing a standard prosthetic on his right shoulder and a thought-controlled robotic arm on his left shoulder, tests the robotic arm's ability to lift a weight. Robotic prosthetics greatly enhance the wearer's ability to move.

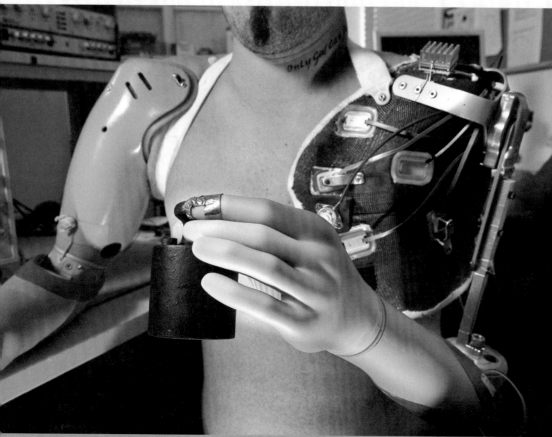

a second. The human brain, on the other hand, has about 100 billion neurons that each may be wired in hundreds of different ways to create about 10 trillion connections. These connections are not simple on/off switches, but complex electrochemical interactions. A memory or an image that reaches a person's consciousness is actually the result of signals arising from whole networks of cells in a way that is still far from clear.

In 2006 Henry Markram and his team at the Swiss Federal Institute of Technology in Lausanne began building a computer that worked more like a brain—a virtual brain of sorts. Using an IBM Blue Gene supercomputer that can perform up to 22 trillion operations per second, they built what amounted to a simulation of a small slice of a brain. Markram believes that the virtual brain slice can be gradually enlarged until it has the size and complexity of a full human brain: "We have achieved the ability to build a brain microcircuit, an elementary unit, and now it's just a matter of scaling up."[9]

Eventually, a virtual brain might help answer one of the most puzzling questions in all of science: how does a brain create the experience of being aware or conscious? Some scientists and philosophers believe that consciousness requires some special, unique interaction of brain, body, and environment. Others suggest that any sufficiently complex network of connections might become conscious—something no computer has yet achieved. Markram suggests, "Once we build the whole brain, if consciousness emerges, we will be able to study it systematically and understand exactly how it emerges."[10]

Chapter TWO

Exploring the Cosmos

Is there life on Mars? What secrets might be hidden beneath the surface of Jupiter's icy moon Europa? Is humanity somehow alone in the cosmos, or might there be another planet like Earth circling some distant star? While these questions were not definitively answered in the 2000s, scientists found tantalizing clues, aided by a fleet of space-going robots and powerful new telescopes.

The giant planets of Jupiter and Saturn and their intriguing moons were a major focus of the decade's space exploration efforts. Arriving at Jupiter in 1995, the *Galileo* space probe had taken the long way around—getting gravitational boosts by flying by Venus and Earth. Shortly after its arrival, *Galileo* launched its own probe into Jupiter's atmosphere to measure its composition. In early 2002 *Galileo* completed its observations of Io, a strange moon covered with active volcanoes that send plumes of material far into space. *Galileo* also extensively explored Jupiter's moon Europa, finding evidence for a vast ocean under an icy surface. In September 2002 *Galileo* was sent on a final plunge into Jupiter's atmosphere to avoid the possibly of it contaminating Europa with Earth organisms. In 2004 it was Saturn's turn for a visit. The international *Cassini-Huygens* mission consisted of two spacecraft: an orbiter and a lander. *Cassini* entered a complex orbit around Saturn, adjusting as necessary to enable it to repeatedly fly close to Titan, Saturn's largest moon. Gradually, using special light filters and radar, a somewhat detailed picture of the moon's surface was revealed.

In January 2005 the *Huygens* lander entered Titan's atmosphere and descended to the surface by parachute. The scientists did not know, however, just what sort of surface might be encountered—hills, flat land, or even a lake or ocean. About 350 pictures taken from the surface and relayed via the orbiting *Cassini* revealed the landing spot to have hills of ice and gullies where torrential rains of hydrocarbon-laced water may drain. *Huygens* represented a milestone in the ability to land on and obtain data from bodies in the outer reaches of the solar system. Another sort of milestone was achieved in 2006 when the *Stardust* probe returned to Earth with samples of dust it had scooped from a comet—the first material ever returned from beyond the Moon's orbit.

Perhaps the most spectacular space achievements of the decade, however, came from a visit to a neighboring planet—Mars. In January 2004 two rovers, *Spirit* and *Opportunity*, successfully landed on Mars. Their names had been submitted in a NASA contest by Sofi Collis, a nine-year-old girl who was born in Siberia but adopted by an American family. In her essay, she wrote, "I used to live in an orphanage. It was dark and cold and lonely. At night, I looked up at the sparkly sky and felt better. I dreamed I could fly there. In America, I can make all my dreams come true. Thank you for the 'Spirit' and the 'Opportunity.'"[11]

Robotic Rovers Reach Mars

The atmosphere in the NASA control room early in the morning of January 4, 2004, was almost unbearably intense. The mission controllers knew that getting anything to Mars, let alone landing two complicated machines on the planet's surface, was far from a sure thing. Only months earlier two Mars probes, the Japanese orbiter *Nozomi* and the British lander *Beagle 2* had gone silent and were presumed lost.

As the *Spirit* lander began to streak through the atmosphere of Mars at thousands of miles an hour, everything would have to go exactly right. The outer cover, or aeroshell, would have to slow the vehicle down without burning up. Once the shell was released, a parachute would have to slow the descent still more as the atmosphere became thicker. Finally, retrorockets would need to fire until, at a height of 30 feet (9 m), air bags much like those found in a car would cushion the final drop of the Mars rover to the surface.

There was literally nothing the controllers could do during the six-minute landing. Even if they could have sent instructions to the

This stunning view of Saturn was taken by the orbiter Cassini *in 2004. Hundreds of other images taken by the lander* Huygens *on the surface of Saturn's largest moon, Titan, were transmitted to scientists on Earth by* Cassini.

spacecraft, the radio waves would not have reached Mars in time to make a difference. They could only wait for the signals that might carry the news of a successful landing—or the silence that would suggest a problem.

People Should Go to Mars

Sending people to Mars would be exciting, but also expensive and risky. In recent years advocates of human space exploration have clashed with scientists who believe the money would be better spent on robotic probes and rovers.

Buzz Aldrin—the second human to walk on the moon, after Neil Armstrong—believes that Mars is the next destination for astronauts that makes sense "from a scientific, technology-advancing, meaningful, and politically inspiring point of view." It would be a fitting follow-up to the moon program, which, according to Aldrin, "symbolized the ability of this nation to conceive a truly pathbreaking idea, prioritize it, create the technology to advance the idea, and then ride it to completion."

Another longtime supporter of human exploration of Mars is aerospace engineer and writer Robert Zubrin. Zubrin, founder of the Mars Society (a group that studies and promotes Mars exploration), has worked out a detailed scheme for the settlement of Mars. Instead of building the huge, expensive spaceships needed to go there and back, Zubrin's more economical space program would first land chemical plants on the planet. These would process liquid hydrogen brought from Earth with carbon dioxide extracted from the Martian atmosphere, producing methane and oxygen to fuel both surface vehicles and the trip back to Earth. The first Mars explorers would build the basic structures needed for a small town. Living and working on the planet would bring knowledge and experience that no brief visit by a robot could obtain.

Buzz Aldrin, *Mission to Mars: My Vision for Space Exploration*. Washington, DC: *National Geographic*, 2013, p. 26.

Finally, the mission controllers heard an announcement on the loud-speaker: "We have a signal indicating bouncing on the surface."[12] NASA's Mission Control Center erupted as pent-up tension turned to cheers, leaps, and hugs. Sometime later the *Spirit* rover detached from its air-bags, opened its solar-cell "wings," and transmitted the first picture from the Martian surface. Steve Squyres, lead scientist for the mission, could only mutter, "It works, man. It works."[13] About three weeks later, the controllers had another round of nail-biting suspense as *Spirit*'s twin, a rover called *Opportunity*, touched down on the other side of the planet.

Driving on Mars

Mars is strikingly like Earth in some ways. At its warmest it is like a cool day on Earth, though nighttime temperatures plunge to Antarctic levels. Much of the landscape looks remarkably similar to the most barren parts of the deserts of the southwestern United States, only more red. Driving a rover on Mars, however, is nothing like setting off on a freewheeling road trip across the Southwest. Since it takes fifteen

PERSPECTIVES

Let Robots Explore Mars

Whether envisioned as a big push like the Apollo moon program of the 1960s or a gradual buildup of the capability of humans to travel beyond the moon, sending people to Mars would be a major undertaking costing tens of billions of dollars and spanning decades. Science writer Lawrence M. Krauss believes that robots should be the first to explore Mars. He notes that

> we have sent robots to places humans never could have survived and peered into the cosmos with instruments far more capable than our human senses, all for a small fraction of the cost to send a living, breathing person into Earth's orbit. The first rovers went to Mars for what it would cost to make a movie about sending [actor] Bruce Willis to Mars. And the Hubble Space Telescope, perhaps the most important and expensive unmanned device sent into space thus far, has captured our imagination in a way the International Space Station never has. And our robotic technology continues to improve.

Krauss believes that humans will one day reach Mars and settle there. The question is whether now is the time to make such an effort given the challenges (both economic and climatic) that science and technology are being asked to tackle here on Earth. For now, he says, it might be better to let increasingly sophisticated robots search for life on Mars or perhaps on the moons of Jupiter and Saturn.

Lawrence M. Krauss, "Rethinking the Dream of Human Spaceflight," *Scientific American*, April 5, 2011. www.scientific american.com.

minutes or so for any radio signal to travel from Earth to Mars, every-thing has to be planned in advance. After the science teams set their objective (such as a particular rock), the rover driver uses computer simulation to put together a series of commands that, move by move, should get the rover safely to its destination. (They do this during

The rovers Spirit *(depicted in a NASA illustration) and* Opportunity *landed on Mars in 2004. They were powered by solar panels and carried cameras on their masts to provide scientists panoramic views of the planet's surface and tools and microscopes to analyze rock samples.*

the Martian night, while the rover is "sleeping.") They have to watch carefully for possible obstacles or slippery footing, although the rover does have some ability to stop if it senses a problem. If the rover is parked at a site of interest, it may be given a series of commands for the robot arm to take a sample for analysis. When the commands have been repeatedly checked, they are uploaded to the rover as part of a package of activities for the next Mars day. The rover acknowledges the commands, but there is no instant gratification. The anxious scientists on Earth have to wait for the next scheduled batch of data containing the images and measurements to be sent to Earth, usually via the Mars orbiter circling in the sky above.

The two rovers operated as designed—most of the time. But on January 21, 2004, *Spirit's* regular data transmissions stopped abruptly in midstream. Like a faulty desktop computer, the rover rebooted itself over and over. Unlike a desktop computer, troubleshooting involved sending commands and waiting as long as a day to see what *Spirit's* response might be.

Finally, the NASA computer specialists determined that the rover's 256 megabytes of flash memory (similar to a thumb drive) was filling up and being copied into the smaller main memory. This in turn was writing over the rover's operating instructions, causing the crashes. After fixing the problem, NASA lead flight software engineer Robert Denise gave a detailed explanation but finished it up with a simpler answer: "The *Spirit* was willing, but the flash was weak."[14]

The two rovers had only just begun their remarkable careers. By January 2009 they had sent 250,000 images back to Earth, and had traveled more than 13 miles (21 km). Designed to last a minimum of ninety days, both rovers operated into the following decade. *Spirit* eventually got stuck and communication was lost in March 2010. *Opportunity*, however, set out for Mars's Endeavour Crater, a journey that was still continuing in 2013.

Searching for Water (and Life)

Ever since a few observers in the late nineteenth century thought they saw canals crisscrossing the planet's surface, the possibility that Mars might have life has fascinated many people. But scientists could only speculate about the planet's life-giving characteristics. The first successful landing on Mars by NASA's *Viking* spacecraft in 1976 brought new and valuable information about the red planet. The *Viking* mission consisted of two separate spacecraft, each with an orbiter for photographic survey and a lander to study the planet's surface. The photographic and other data obtained greatly expanded knowledge but did not definitively answer the question about life on Mars.

By the 1990s the focus of the Mars missions shifted from direct attempts to detect life to learning more about the composition of Mars—in particular, determining the presence of water, which is considered a vital ingredient for most forms of life. In 2002, scanning from orbit, the *Mars Odyssey* spacecraft detected the likely presence of large underground bodies of water beneath the planet's polar regions. Two years later as the *Spirit* rover slowly made its way out of dry, dusty Gusev Crater and into the Columbia Hills, a different picture emerged. At a March 23, 2004, news conference, NASA announced that the rover had found both geological and chemical evidence that pointed to a Mars that once had abundant flowing surface water. Meanwhile *Opportunity*, exploring the small crater in which it had landed, found layered or sedimentary rocks containing minerals that typically result from the evaporation of a salty body of water.

Scientists believe that Mars still has water on its surface—mainly in the form of ice at the planet's poles. In 2008 NASA guided the *Phoenix* lander to an area near the Martian north pole. When the lander's robot scoop dug a trench in the nearby soil, the camera picked up bits of reflective, glinting material. Was it ice, or perhaps only a kind of salt? The fact that the glints soon disappeared convinced scientists that it was indeed ice that had melted when exposed to the sun. Using a robot arm, the researchers scooped up a sample and found that, when heated, it released water vapor. The confirmation of water on Mars raised hopes that some form of life might exist on the planet. Further, it suggested that future Mars colonists might be able to thrive there.

Private Rockets and Tourist Spaceships

In 2001 Dennis Tito got to do something only a few hundred human beings have ever done. He boarded a Russian *Soyuz* capsule for a ride up to the International Space Station. After spending a week viewing Earth from the orbiting platform and conducting some scientific experiments, he returned safely to Earth.

Tito was not an astronaut, however. At the time of his journey into space, he was a successful engineer turned technology investment manager, and his trip cost him about $20 million. By the end of the decade, seven "space tourists" (including South African entrepreneur Mark Shuttleworth, Microsoft developer Charles Simonyi, and game designer Richard Garriott) had given a small boost to a new industry—commercial space travel. Since these first space tourists had to fly with astronauts in a small, aging capsule and join a working space station, they underwent extensive training. Being in space also took some getting used to, as Simonyi (who made two flights) recalled: "The *Soyuz* is put into a constant rotation so that the solar panels face the sun. Looking at the earth while the spacecraft is rotating can get you sick. You can get sick even if you don't look at the earth. . . . So for the first couple of orbits we weren't supposed to look at the earth."[15]

Space tourism was changing the way people thought about space travel. The space programs that had sent Russian and American astronauts into orbit, reached the moon, and operated space stations such as Mir and the International Space Station were all operated by governments. The specially trained astronauts generally were former military pilots. While NASA's rockets and other systems were built by private companies, and communications satellites were a thriving industry, actual human space flight remained a government monopoly.

Private Companies Develop Spacecraft

This began to change during the 2000s. Space flight enthusiasts had long pointed out that the rapid development of aviation in the first decades of the twentieth century was due to a successful mix of government and private initiatives. The federal government had paid for pilots to carry air mail, while individuals such as the publisher William Randolph Hearst had offered prizes for the first aviator to make a particular flight. Inspired by this tradition, in 1996 the XPRIZE Foundation offered a $10 million prize for the first nongovernmental organization to launch a reusable manned spacecraft into space twice within two weeks. (The idea was to demonstrate that spacecraft could operate on a regular schedule like airliners). In October 2004 the space plane *SpaceShipOne*, designed by

SpaceShipOne—*the first privately developed and piloted vehicle to reach space—sits on a runway in California's Mojave Desert. In 2004 the rocket-powered spacecraft briefly ascended into space and then glided safely back to Earth.*

aerospace engineer Burt Rutan, won the prize by completing two brief suborbital flights.

Increasingly, NASA wanted to focus its future efforts on space exploration and scientific research, not routine transportation. Thus, the government began to offer incentives and contracts to companies willing to develop and operate vehicles to deliver cargoes and people to orbit. In 2002 a company called SpaceX was founded by PayPal entrepreneur Elon Musk. During the 2000s SpaceX developed the Falcon rockets and Dragon capsules that began to deliver supplies to the International Space Station in 2012. Meanwhile, both SpaceX and billionaire entrepreneur Richard Branson's Virgin Galactic began to develop spaceships that could carry people on excursion flights to the edge of space and eventually into orbit. Perhaps, looking back, the 2000s will turn out to be to space travel what the 1920s were to aviation.

The Search for Another Earth

Exobiologists (scientists who study life on other planets) have a problem—it is hard to study something when there is only one sample of it. The only planet *known* to have life is Earth. However, if there are millions of stars similar to Earth's sun, it might be reasonable to assume that they, too, have systems of planets in orbit around them. If so, medium-sized rocky planets at the right distance from their star are logical candidates to be Earth-like and have water and perhaps life.

Until the 1990s this was all theory, since no planets had actually been detected around even the nearest stars. All at once, however, two ingenious techniques were used to reveal a growing number of exoplanets—that is, planets outside of Earth's solar system. The more common method relies on gravity and light. One thinks of planets as orbiting around stars, but it is more accurate to say that they orbit together around their gravitational center. This means the star itself is moving in a regular way. Using a very sensitive spectrograph, changes in the wavelength of light can be measured as the planet's gravity drags the star first toward and then away from an observer on Earth. (This change in the light is similar to how the pitch of the siren's sound changes as a fire truck approaches and then passes the listener.) Sometimes planets can also be detected as they pass in front of a star and block part of its light—an eclipse.

What is it like to measure something that involves such a tiny, subtle change? Astronomer Steve Vogt noted that "if you took a metal ruler a couple of inches long, and then stood it on end, the amount it would shrink due to gravity is the kind of effect you're trying to measure. If you picked it up, the expansion due to heat from your hand is a hundred times *more* than the effect you're looking for. And you've got to measure that."[16]

Because exoplanets are easier to detect by either light or gravitational effects, the earliest ones found were giants, balls of gas the size of Jupiter or larger. However, in February 2009 a European group led by two French researchers used the Corot space telescope (which was designed specifically to detect exoplanets) to observe a star, Corot-7, about five hundred light-years away. They observed a tiny dimming of the star's light (less than one-thirtieth of 1 percent) that indicated that a planet about twice the diameter of Earth was passing between the telescope and the star. Measurements of the planet's gravitational influence on its star suggest that it is a rocky planet like Earth. It is no place for life, though—it is much too close to its star, giving it a surface temperature of about 2,000°F (1,093°C). Nevertheless, the discovery demonstrated that the planet hunters were starting to find planets that, if placed in a more hospitable orbit, might be quite like Earth.

Once an exoplanet is found, what more can be learned about it? In 2008 astronomers detected methane (an organic compound best known on Earth as the main component of natural gas) in the atmosphere of a Jupiter-sized exoplanet. They also found water. While this planet was likely both too big and too hot to harbor life, these results showed the beginning of an ability to determine whether any such distant planet has the necessary ingredients for life.

Getting the Picture

Stories about exoplanets are often accompanied by illustrations by artists of what such planets might look like, because photographs are nearly impossible to obtain. Science writer Ray Jayawardhana imagines what someone on a distant planet would have to do to be able to see Earth's solar system: "For an alien photographer that wants to capture a family portrait of our solar system from tens of light years away, the challenge would be akin to catching a glimpse of a few fireflies right next to a bright searchlight from a distance of 1,000 kilometers."[17]

It took technology, skill, and some luck to get the first actual pictures of other worlds. In 2008 a team of astronomers was able to use the Hubble Space Telescope to photograph not one but three planets in orbit around the star Fomalhaut, about twenty-five light-years away. These planets were all hot and much bigger than Jupiter, which helped them show up in the infrared images. One team member, astrophysicist Bruce Macintosh of the Lawrence Livermore National Laboratory, sounded exuberant when he stated, "Every extrasolar planet detected so far has been a wobble on a graph. These are the first pictures of an entire system. We've been trying to image planets for eight years with no luck and now we have pictures of three planets at once."[18]

Chapter THREE

Mysteries of Energy and Matter

In the 2000s researchers took advantage of new technologies to explore the fundamental nature of matter both on Earth and in the cosmos. The fruits of research into the tiny realm of atoms and particles in turn began to appear in new products and technologies. Sometimes research crossed traditional boundaries, such as when computer scientists and engineers began to use phenomena from quantum physics and even biology to design powerful new kinds of computers. Another important feature of science and technology in the new century was the increasing importance of international cooperation for building massive research facilities such as the Large Hadron Collider.

The World's Biggest Machine

The Large Hadron Collider (LHC) is the biggest machine ever built. Straddling the border of France and Switzerland near the city of Geneva, it is 17 miles (27 km) in circumference and buried as much as 574 feet (175 m) in the ground. It has a network, or grid, of tens of thousands of computers to deal with the data generated by dozens of experiments—about 15 million gigabytes of data a year. Built by the European Organization for Nuclear Research (CERN) at a cost of more than $9 billion, its purpose is to crack open the deep structure of physical reality by slamming particles together with incredible energy. To reach that goal, CERN employs thousands of scientists, engineers, technicians, and other workers from more than sixty countries.

The collision process begins with protons stripped from hydrogen atoms, or heavier lead ions can be used. These particles are first given a boost by a series of smaller accelerators and then injected into the LHC itself. To propel the beams around the huge circle requires 1,232 magnets. Another 392 magnets are needed to keep the beams focused. The magnets each weigh almost 30 tons (27 metric tons). To gain their power, the magnets are cooled to a temperature near absolute zero, making them superconductive. Keeping them cool requires four huge refrigerators, about 100 tons (91 metric tons) of liquid helium, and a lot of cables. In fact, if all the cables that make up the LHC's plumbing were laid end to end, they would reach from Earth to the sun five times.

The LHC is the largest scientific project ever undertaken, and it represents a milestone in international cooperation. The components for the LHC came from many places. Hundreds of magnets and other components came from Russia, a leading country in high-energy physics. Japan's contributions included a magnet that is used to measure the momentum of particles. Germany, Netherlands, Italy, and Spain built casings and coils for the huge particle detector called ALICE. Companies around the world were given contracts and instructions needed to build hundreds of magnets. Given the scope and complexity of the project, it is not surprising that construction of the LHC (which began in 1998) took most of the 2000s to complete. Indeed Peter Limon, an American researcher working at the LHC, told a visiting writer, "I think this is the most complicated thing that humans have ever built."[19]

Physics at the Intersections

The LHC contains four huge underground caverns, each located at a point where two beams traveling around the ring of pipes will intersect. At each intersection is a detector designed to search for particular kinds of data in particle collisions. Two general purpose detectors, called ATLAS and CMS, are designed to explore the physics of very high energies. One of their first targets would be the Higgs boson, a particle believed to be responsible for giving everything in the universe its mass.

In addition to the two big general purpose detectors, the specialized detector called ALICE seeks to explore quark-gluon plasma. This is a mysterious form of ultra-dense matter that existed immediately after the indescribable chaos that led to the formation of the universe, an event known as the Big Bang. Understanding this material might mean understanding how the universe emerged and perhaps reveal the secret of the hidden dark matter that seems to make up about a quarter of the mass

A technician walks under a massive core magnet being used in a CERN experiment in the Large Hadron Collider, an enormous underground ring used by scientists to find out what happens when beams of particles collide. Successful tests in 2009 promised many new discoveries in the years to come.

in the universe. The fourth detector, LHCb, seeks to find out what happened to the antimatter that was created along with an equal amount of regular matter in the Big Bang.

Other results of planned LHC experiments may reveal whether there are hidden dimensions (beyond the familiar three of length, width, and depth) as predicted by string theory. Or such experiments might fill in the gaps in the so-called Standard Model, the current theory that tries to tie together the fundamental forces of nature. It is hard even for the physicists to imagine what else might be discovered. As French physicist Yves Schutz observed: "We don't even know what to expect. We're now in a domain of energy that nobody has ever explored."[20]

The physicists had eagerly planned enough experiments to last for years, but first they had to find out whether the LHC would operate as expected. On September 10, 2008, the LHC was ready for its first test, which involved firing a beam of protons through one segment of the tunnel at a time. They then successfully sent a beam completely around the tunnel. However, a little over a week later, as testing continued, something went wrong. An electrical fault had caused a power discharge that led to about 6 tons (5.4 metric tons) of liquid helium spewing into the tunnel, damaging fifty superconducting magnets. It was a serious setback, and it took more than a year to fix the damage. However, in November 2009 the LHC successfully completed its tests, smashing particles together at the highest energy ever achieved—1.18 trillion electron volts. At the end of the 2000s, physicists stood on the brink of a new realm of discovery.

Searching for Dark Matter

Sometimes scientists can predict future discoveries. Back in the 1840s astronomers noticed that the planet Uranus, discovered about half a century earlier, was not moving quite as predicted by the laws of orbital mechanics. The British astronomer John Couch Adams and French astronomer Urbain Le Verrier independently calculated that some unknown body must be exerting gravitational force that was distorting the orbit of Uranus. As a result they discovered the planet Neptune.

Dark matter represents a similar problem on a larger—indeed cosmic—scale. Since the late twentieth century, astronomers and astrophysicists had been trying to explain how galaxies or clusters of galaxies formed and took the shapes that have been observed. The problem was that the amount of matter they could observe—whether through optical or radio telescopes—was not enough to account for the gravity needed to pull things into place.

For most scientists of the 2000s, the most plausible explanation was that much of the matter in the universe—perhaps as much as 90 percent—is invisible. It is not just invisible to the human eye; it does not emit any wavelength of radiation at all. This seemingly necessary but currently undetectable mass was dubbed "dark matter." It prompted many questions, including what it might be made of. One possibility is that some dark matter (called hot dark matter) moving near the speed of light, might consist of neutrinos. These ghostly particles, which pass through masses the size of Earth with ease, have an almost indiscernible mass. If there are enough of them, though, they might be part of the dark matter answer. Another part of the answer may be found in cold dark matter, which consists of particles that are not yet known but may be generated in machines such as the LHC.

Looking to the Cosmos for Clues

Scientists did not have to wait for results from the LHC, however. They could look to the cosmos, where nature provides subtle clues. In 2006 a team of researchers observed a collision between two massive clusters of galaxies 3 billion light-years from Earth. First they took images from

---

The Age of International Science

The 2000s decade saw the development of two huge international science projects—the International Space Station and the Large Hadron Collider. In November 2000 the first crew arrived at the space station, which continued to expand as new components were lifted into orbit. During this same time, construction of the world's most powerful particle smasher got under way.

These two megaprojects had unsuccessful American predecessors. In the late 1980s President Ronald Reagan's administration proposed a largely American-built space station called Freedom. However, by 1993, with a new administration in the White House, the unwillingness of Congress to provide funding, and the end of Cold War competition with Russia, the project was canceled.

Meanwhile, the United States had begun to build a physics megaproject— the Superconducting Super Collider. This particle accelerator would have been a ring 54.1 miles (87.1 km) in diameter, pushing protons to a collision energy of 40 trillion electron volts. As cost estimates soared from $4.4 billion to more than $12 billion, and questions were raised about its management, Congress lost enthusiasm for the project and canceled it in 1993.

The fate of these projects suggested that truly large science projects might be beyond the reach of any one nation, particularly in the age of economic austerity that began toward the end of the 2000s. Physicist Steven Weinberg notes, "Big science is in competition for government funds, not only with manned space flight, and with various programs of real science, but also with many other things we need government to do."

Steven Weinberg, "The Crisis of Big Science," *New York Review of Books*, May 10, 2012. www.nybooks.com.

X-rays being emitted by the distant objects. They then measured how much the light was being bent as it passed through the galaxies. Since gravity curves space and bends light (as first described by physicist Albert Einstein), this measurement gave a total mass for the galaxies.

Two spiral galaxies in the Hercules galaxy cluster, located about 450 million light-years from Earth, crash into each other in this remarkable view captured by the orbiting Hubble Space Telescope. Such collisions are of interest to scientists studying dark matter.

The light measurement indicated that there was much more mass than could be accounted for by the X-ray image. Says astrophysicist Marusa Bradac, "This tells us there must be something there, and that is dark matter."[21] Further, the process of collision served to separate the two kinds of matter. Regular matter is slowed down as it is pushed together, but dark matter continues without obstruction. Thus, Bradac noted, "The visible matter creates a sort of traffic jam in the middle, whereas dark matter has its own highway."[22]

Dark Energy

If it is possible for there to be something more mysterious than dark matter, then dark energy is surely a good candidate. Starting in 1998 cosmologist Adam Riess began to observe distant supernovae with the Hubble Space Telescope and ground-based instruments. By peering farther and farther into space, the observers were able to measure the size of the universe at succeeding points in time. Riess recalled, "We anticipated finding that gravity had slowed the rate of expansion over time. But that's not what we found."[23]

Instead, they determined that the expansion rate of the cosmos began to speed up between 5 and 6 billion years ago. This is consistent with dark energy starting to overcome the gravitational forces of regular and dark matter. "After we subtract the gravity from the known matter in the universe, we can see the dark energy pushing to get out,"[24] remarked Hubble science team member Lou Strolger.

In the early 2000s the measurement of microwave energy left over from the Big Bang (using a detector carried aloft by balloons in Antarctica) confirmed Riess's measurements.

What is the long-term impact of this discovery on physics? Riess noted:

One of the most exciting things about dark energy is that it seems to live at the very nexus of two of our most successful theories of physics: quantum mechanics, which explains the physics of the small, and Einstein's Theory of General Relativity, which explains the physics of the large, including gravity. Currently, physicists have to choose between those two theories when they calculate something. Dark energy is giving us a peek into how to make those two theories operate together. Nature somehow must know how to bring these both together, and it is giving us some important clues. It's up to us to figure out what [those clues] are saying.[25]

Traces of the Beginning

When the Big Bang occurred billions of years ago, the emerging universe was extremely hot and consisted only of intense radiation. As the universe expanded, it cooled, and the radiation condensed into subatomic particles and eventually into atoms. The remaining radiation also cooled, and it is now found in the form of microwaves with a very low temperature, just a few degrees above absolute zero.

This cosmic background radiation was predicted by the Big Bang theory, and when it was detected in 1965 it was a major confirmation for that theory. But could this leftover "fossil" radiation reveal anything about the structure of the early universe? The problem is that the radiation is very uniform, seeming to change only imperceptibly as one points a radio telescope at different parts of the sky. A very sensitive detector is needed to measure the anisotropies, or tiny temperature differences in the radiation background.

On June 30, 2001, the *Wilkinson Microwave Anisotropy Probe* (WMAP) was launched. Unlike most satellites, the WMAP was placed in a location called Lagrange 2, about 930,000 miles (1.5 million km) from Earth. In this position, the sun's and Earth's gravity balance so that the spacecraft maintains a constant position relative to the two bodies, minimizing fluctuations in heat that interfere with observations. The observation process was complex. In order to reveal the differences in the background radiation, five different frequencies were compared, and foreground emissions from sources within and beyond our galaxy were subtracted. On February 11, 2003, NASA released the stunning results of the first year's observations, together with a map showing the distribution of the background radiation. According to NASA, it was "the best 'baby picture' of the Universe ever taken, which contains such stunning detail that it may be one of the most important scientific results of recent years."[26]

Managing Technological Risk

In April 2000 Bill Joy, a pioneering computer scientist, published an essay titled "Why the Future Doesn't Need Us." Joy was concerned that "the 21st-century technologies—genetics, nanotechnology, and robotics (GNR)—are so powerful that they can spawn whole new classes of accidents and abuses. Most dangerously, for the first time, these accidents and abuses are widely within the reach of individuals or small groups."

By the end the decade, it was getting easier for people to tinker with genes, thanks to substantial decreases in costs of genetic analysis and laboratory equipment for manipulating genes. Likewise during this period, nanotechnologists were looking to build tiny machines that could use raw materials in the environment to build more such machines, an endeavor that gave rise to concerns about machines capable of reproducing uncontrollably.

Perhaps Joy's biggest concern was that new technologies promised immediate benefits, but their risks might not be known for some time. "With each of these technologies, a sequence of small, individually sensible advances leads to an accumulation of great power and, concomitantly, great danger."

Responding to Joy's essay, inventor and futurist Ray Kurzweil asked whether people "should cancel the development of all bioengineered treatments because there is a risk that these same technologies be used for malevolent purposes."

The question remains: how can society encourage innovation while developing appropriate oversight and regulation? Perhaps a first step is becoming informed about new technologies and reflecting on one's own role in developing or using them.

Bill Joy, "Why the Future Doesn't Need Us," *Wired*, April 2000. www.wired.com.

Ray Kurzweil, *The Singularity Is Near: When Humans Transcend Biology*. New York: Penguin, 2006, p. 407.

The precise new measurements fixed the age of the universe at 13.77 billion years. There were also new discoveries. It turned out that the birth of the first generation of stars was only 200 million years after the Big Bang, much earlier than most scientists had assumed. There was also further confirmation of the validity of the Big Bang theory itself, as well as the idea of inflation—the extremely rapid expansion of the newborn universe that accounts for the general uniformity of space and time.

Finally, there was a strong boost to the belief of most scientists that dark matter and dark energy must exist even though they are, so far, undetectable. The "census" of the universe was determined to be 4 percent regular matter (atoms and particles), 23 percent dark matter, and 73 percent dark energy. NASA astronomy and physics director Anne Kinney noted in the same press release, "These numbers represent a milestone in how we view our Universe. This is a true turning point for cosmology."[27]

Nanotechnology: The Surprising Power of Small

As scientists learned more about strange kinds of matter in the cosmos, researchers were also learning how to manipulate atoms in new ways here on Earth. Nanotechnology is the ability to create or arrange matter directly at the atomic or molecular level. Writing in 2006, Mihail C. Roco, senior nanotechnology adviser for the National Science Foundation, noted, "Today nanotechnology is still in a formative phase—not unlike the condition of computer science in the 1960s or biotechnology in the 1980s. Yet it is maturing rapidly. Between 1997 and 2005, investment in nanotech research and development by governments around the world soared from $432 million to about $4.1 billion."[28]

One basic advantage of using tiny nanoparticles for chemical interactions is that they greatly increase the available surface area of the substance. (Consider, for example, how much faster crushed ice will cool a drink compared to the same quantity of ice cubes). As a result, catalysts, substances that promote a chemical process, can be made to be much more efficient. Today hundreds of millions of automobiles use catalytic converters containing expensive platinum or palladium to reduce smog and other harmful emissions. In 2007 Mazda Motor Corporation revealed a catalytic converter using nanoparticles. By using nanoparticles, they reduced the use of precious metals by 70 to 90 percent.

Nanotech Products

By 2009 an inventory of nanotech products kept by the Project on Emerging Nanotechnologies exceeded one thousand items from nearly five hundred companies in more than twenty countries. Most of these applications involve relatively simple, uniform materials such as particles of zinc oxide used for sunscreens, fibers, or wires for specialized electronics. However, more-complex structures were also being built using nanotechnology. One of the most interesting is the carbon nanotube.

Carbon nanotubes are cylinders only one atom thick, but they are incredibly strong. In 2007 a team led by Ali Dhinojwala of the Polymer Science Department at the University of Akron in Ohio developed a superstrong tape by growing microfibers from carbon nanotubes. A button-sized piece of the tape can support almost 9 pounds (4 kg) of weight, yet the tape can be easily "unstuck" if desired. The tape even conducts heat and radiates it away, a useful property for designers of devices. In 2009 Dhinojwala and one of his graduate students formed a company to develop commercial applications. Meanwhile, in 2008 Samsung demonstrated a

A close-up view of a carbon nanotube shows its cylindrical structure. In 2007 researchers developed a superstrong tape by growing microfibers from carbon nanotubes.

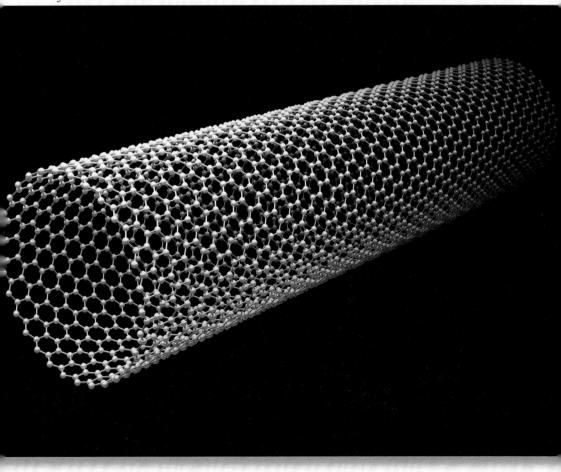

form of electronic paper display (similar to that used in Kindles and other e-reader devices) using carbon nanotubes. The resulting thin, light screens have advantages for mobile devices such as phones, e-readers, and even wristwatches. Designers began to consider a variety of other applications for nanotubes. When added to textiles, they could be used to make waterproof or tear-resistant fabrics or versatile body armor. Used in plastics, they could make cars that are lighter and more fuel efficient without sacrificing protection for passengers.

Computing Beyond Silicon

Advances in understanding and manipulating matter during the 2000s also offered new technological possibilities that could make computers vastly more powerful. Anyone who buys a new computer every few years knows that each new machine is considerably faster and has more memory than the old one. Back in 1965 Gordon Moore, founder of the computer-chip maker Intel, observed that about every two years the processing power of computer circuits doubled because more components could be fit into a given space. Remarkably, the trend, called Moore's Law, has continued for almost five decades. For example, the fastest supercomputer in 1999 could perform about 1 trillion operations per second. By 2008 Roadrunner, an IBM supercomputer at the Los Alamos National Laboratory, had broken the barrier of 1 quadrillion operations per second.

Moore's Law may not hold true forever. Throughout the 2000s chip designers found ways to make components smaller or space them closer together, but two problems are looming. First, all those components produce heat, and it becomes increasingly difficult to keep the processor cool enough to operate reliably. Also, in the increasingly tiny dimensions involved in the latest chips, the laws of quantum mechanics come into play, allowing electrons to escape from the circuit. In 2012 Michio Kaku, one of the world's leading physicists, wrote, "In about ten years or so, we will see the collapse of Moore's Law. In fact . . . already we see a slowing down of Moore's Law. Computer power simply cannot maintain its rapid exponential rise using standard silicon technology."[29]

There are various means to continue improving computer performance, such as finding better ways to link large numbers of computers (or individual processors) together or building circuits that take more advantage of the third dimension instead of being mostly flat. However, researchers of the 2000s began to work on entirely different forms of computer processors that do not use silicon integrated circuits at all.

Building a Quantum Computer

Rather than limiting the advance of computers, quantum effects are being used to design computers vastly smaller and more powerful than conventional machines. Unlike a conventional computer, where each bit (the smallest unit of data) can have only one state (either a one or a zero), a quantum bit, or qubit, can be represented by atoms that, by the rules of quantum mechanics, can have multiple energy states. This allows them to represent many numbers at the same time. This means that a quantum computer can potentially perform a vast number of calculations simultaneously.

The problem is that this special quantum situation, called a superposition, is extremely fragile. The very attempt to read the data usually destroys it—a phenomenon called decoherence. Another quantum phenomenon, called entanglement, can be used to link multiple atoms representing the same data, to try to ensure that the data can still be read.

A working, full-scale quantum computer would revolutionize every aspect of computing. (It could also be used to crack just about any form of encryption—a real concern for government and business.) Until recently, though, researchers could only demonstrate a few very simple calculations. However, in 2009 a team based at Yale University built an electronic quantum processor that could fit into an actual computer. Yale professor Robert Schoelkopf explained, "Our processor can perform only a few quantum tasks, which have been demonstrated before with single nuclei, atoms, and photons. But this is the first time they've been possible in an all-electronic device that feels much more like a regular microprocessor."[30]

A Living Computer

Another route to even faster computing may be as close as the cells that make up the human body. DNA encodes the information needed to build an organism, but now that scientists have the ability to synthesize DNA, it can be made to represent computer data or code instead of biological instructions. In 2002 researchers at the Weizmann Institute of Science in Rehovot, Israel, demonstrated a computer that uses DNA and enzymes instead of silicon chips. Combining the right instructions with the enzymes results in chemical reactions that can carry out calculations, sort data, or even look for patterns. Since millions of DNA molecules can fit into a tiny space, all calculating at the same time, the result is a computer that can perform 330 trillion operations per second. While not yet as versatile as an electronic digital computer, DNA computers have the advantage of meshing with biological systems. Ehud Shapiro, leader of the Israeli DNA-computing team, suggested that someday, "autonomous bio-molecular computers may be able to work as 'doctors in a cell,' operating inside living cells and sensing anomalies in the host. Consulting their programmed medical knowledge, the computers could respond to anomalies by synthesizing and releasing drugs."[31]

Developments in new ways of computing, like advances in nanotechnology, showed how science and technology in the 2000s depended on one another to make progress. Without the discoveries of physicists and materials scientists, it would be hard to develop truly new technologies. At the same time, without ever-growing computing power and innovative instruments, scientists could not perform the increasingly complex and sensitive experiments needed to unlock the secrets of matter.

From the farthest reaches of the cosmos to the tiniest bits of matter here on Earth, scientists and engineers of the 2000s were busy exploring new frontiers—and building new machines to reach even further.

Chapter FOUR

Going Mobile and Getting Social

New computing devices such as smartphones and e-readers were introduced during the 2000s. However the most significant digital developments of the decade did not involve new devices, but rather, new ways of using the web. A variety of new forms of online communications and social networking changed the way people used technology—and how they related to one another.

During the 2000s, high-speed broadband technology over cable and phone lines expanded the ways people could use the Internet. For example, it made it practicable for people to listen to music and watch videos online. There was a problem, however. Users could not keep up with the explosion of new web pages being created every day. Someone using one of the simple search programs of the late 1990s could get a list of pages that matched particular keywords, but the list did not do a good job of indicating which pages were most likely to be relevant.

Enter two Stanford graduate students, Larry Page and Sergey Brin. Their search engine used a new algorithm called PageRank, and it was the heart of a new company called Google. In a 1998 paper, Page and Brin described how the algorithm works:

> PageRank relies on the uniquely democratic nature of the web by using its vast link structure as an indicator of an individual page's value. In essence, Google interprets a link from page A to page B as a vote, by page A, for page B. But, Google looks at considerably more than the sheer volume of votes . . . it also analyzes the page that casts the vote. Votes cast by pages that are themselves "important" weigh more heavily and help to make other pages "important."[32]

Through the 2000s decade Google combined its superior search strategies with innovative programs to match advertisers with the people who were most likely to be interested in their products. High-speed communications had made the web fast, and Google made it more useful. The next step was to make the web truly accessible anytime and anywhere.

Apple Goes Mobile

In June 2007 blogger Harry McCracken posted the following as hundreds of people lined up to wait for hours just to have a chance to buy an expensive new cell phone:

> At about 5:30, the Apple iLine handlers began condensing the line—everyone who'd been sprawled on the sidewalk or stretched out in a chair got up and squinched closer to the store itself.
>
> And then we heard hooting and hollering from behind, which turned out to be an army of seemingly dozens and dozens of Apple Store staffers in Jobsian black shirts [Apple founder Steve Jobs often wore dark turtleneck shirts], who marched past us into the store.
>
> At 6—more or less on the dot—us iPhone buyers started to get let in, in small groups. As the eighty-third person in line, it took awhile before I got in. But once I did, it was one of the most bizarre, Barnumesque [circus-like] experiences of my life.[33]

Apple was one of the earliest makers of personal computers, such as the Apple II and the innovative Macintosh. By the end of the 1990s, however, Apple's sales were in decline. Steve Jobs, who had been forced out of the company earlier, was invited to head it again in 1997. As Jobs's biographer, Walter Isaacson, later noted, "He and his colleagues at Apple were able to think differently: They developed not merely modest product advances based on focus groups, but whole new devices and services that consumers did not yet know they needed."[34]

In October 2001 Apple introduced the iPod, a pocket-sized digital music player. While personal digital music players already existed, they tended to be somewhat hard to use. The iPod had simple controls and could store a thousand songs. The next step was to make it easy to buy music for the device. The result was iTunes and the iTunes Store, introduced in April 2003. By the end of the decade, iTunes was the world's

The Apple iPhone, introduced in 2007, had only one button on the front and everything—including typing—could be done by touch. The phone built on Apple's experience with the iPod MP3 player and the company's user-friendly interfaces.

most popular music store; it also sold videos and apps (small programs, often for portable devices).

Technology Giants

The next "i" innovation was the iPhone, introduced in June 2007. By this time cell phones were nothing new. But the iPhone drew upon Apple's experience with the iPod and user interfaces. The iPhone had only one button on the front—everything including typing could be done simply by touch. The phone included a web browser, and soon the ability to install apps was added. By the end of the 2000 decade, the iPhone 4 offered a 5 megapixel camera that could also shoot video, built-in motion sensors, GPS for maps and location-based services, and a store with several hundred thousand apps.

However, Apple soon met with competition from another technology giant: Google. While Apple was revolutionizing mobile devices and user interfaces, Google had turned a state-of-the-art search engine into an empire of information. Google grew rapidly through the 2000s, acquiring new technologies and services—for example, buying the vastly popular YouTube in 2006. All of these information services made Google a powerful player in the mobile market. In 2007 (the same year as Apple's iPhone came out) Google unveiled Android, a Linux-based operating system that can be freely used by manufacturers and programmers. By the end of 2010, Android had become the most widely used smartphone operating system and offered a range of apps comparable to Apple's.

Facebook and the Social Networking Revolution

If the first web revolution of the 2000s aimed to make information organized and accessible, and the second one wanted people to buy things, the third brought families and existing friends together while encouraging an ever-widening circle of personal connections. Thanks to the impact of Facebook and other social networks, by the end of the decade *friend* had joined *google* as a commonly used verb in everyday vocabulary.

By the beginning of the decade, social connections were already being used in innovative ways by online stores. Both Amazon and eBay realized early on that fostering social connections could bring in more customers and increase sales. Amazon encouraged users to post reviews of books. On eBay the feedback buyers and sellers posted about each other could be vital for establishing a good reputation. But while Amazon and eBay saw the value in promoting sales through user comments and interaction, the social networks that emerged in the 2000s represented an even more direct use of people's social connections.

Mark Zuckerberg was a typical bright kid of the computer age, growing up in the 1990s and writing elaborate computer strategy games. As a prep school student, he wrote a program that put together playlists of MP3 music files. Turning down offers from technology companies, including Microsoft, Zuckerberg enrolled at Harvard in 2002. Perhaps surprisingly, given his background, Zuckerberg decided to major not in computer science but in psychology. He later told a writer, "I just think people are the most interesting thing—other people. What it comes down to, for me, is that people want to do what will make them happy, but in order to understand that they really have to understand their world and what is going on around them."[35]

Despite his choice of major, Zuckerberg continued to write programs. Harvard and many other colleges had put together a class directory called a "facebook," with a photo for each student and a brief list of background information and interests. It seemed obvious to Zuckerberg and many other students that something like this should become a website. As Zuckerberg explained later to the *Harvard Crimson*, "Everyone's been talking about a universal face book within Harvard. I think it's kind of silly that it would take the University a couple years to get around to it as I can do it better than they can, and I can do it in a week."[36]

After building the site, called the facebook, Zuckerberg and his roommate Dustin Moskovitz announced it on their dorm's e-mail list. As Moskovitz recalled, "By the end of the night we were . . . actively watching the registration process. Within twenty-four hours, we had somewhere between twelve hundred and fifteen hundred registrants."[37]

Many Uses for Social Networking

The site (later renamed Facebook) quickly spread to dozens of other schools, including Columbia, Yale, and Stanford. By the end of 2004, the site had a quarter million users, and Zuckerberg had gathered enough money from investors and other entrepreneurs to buy enough computers to keep up with the growth of the service. In September 2006 Facebook had opened to anyone more than thirteen years old. By September 2009 the service had over 200 million users worldwide.

People soon found many ways to use Facebook. Users could describe their background and interests in personal profiles, and read others' profiles to find people who shared their interests. It was easy to use one's Facebook page to keep family and friends up to date about such events as vacations, job promotions, or perhaps a new girlfriend or boyfriend. It was also easy to share photos and organize them into albums. In 2006

PERSPECTIVES

Social Networks Are Strengthening Human Relationships

Are people using Facebook and other social media as a substitute for face-to-face relationships? Not according to a 2010 study at the University of Texas–Austin led by media professor S. Craig Watkins. The researchers interviewed nine hundred college students and graduates. They found that "Facebook is not supplanting face-to-face interactions among friends, family and colleagues. In fact, we believe social media afford opportunities for new expressions of friendship, intimacy, and community." The researchers go on to say, "Whether it's a wall post, photo, comment or news link, young people's engagement with Facebook is driven primarily by a desire to stay connected and involved in the lives of family and friends who live near and far, or have recently entered their lives."

In studying graduates, they found that as older people become more fluent in using social networks, they may also be strengthening ties between generations. Referring to the baby boom generation, born between 1946 and 1964, they note: "Using Facebook to strengthen familial ties indicates that boomer parents are now quite active, leading us to believe that the generational gap in social media use is closing."

Quoted in "Social Media Actually Strengthen Social Ties, Various Demographics Engage Differently, Study Says," Phys.Org, November 25, 2010. http://phys.org.

Social Networks Are Fragmenting Human Relationships

Are people making more friends online but having fewer truly satisfying friendships? What is happening to the ability of friends or family members to spend quality time together? Sherry Turkle, a psychologist at Massachusetts Institute of Technology, is concerned about what social networks, particularly when combined with mobile devices, are doing to personal interaction and relationships. Says Turkle,

> "I think so many of us are starting to realize that something is going amiss when we have dinner with friends and everyone has a phone on the table and interrupts conversations in order to take those calls. When everyone is answering emails instead of talking to colleagues at work, something is going amiss."

The fragmented attention brought about by technology may also be affecting peoples' ability to focus, concentrate, or reflect on their own thoughts. Turkle explains:

> I think that one of the things that is being lost is the ability to tolerate solitude. In my own studies I call it, "I share, therefore I am." That is to say, you go from a position where you say "I have a feeling, I want to make a call," to a position where you say "I want to have a feeling, I need to send a text." So what's being lost is the ability to experience your thoughts and feelings without immediately sharing them and you lose the capacity to collaborate. . . . You need to come to collaboration with a sense of self, with your own ideas and confidence in yourself.

Quoted in Simon Mainwaring, "Sherry Turkle of MIT: The Human Cost of Social Technology," *The We First Blog*, September 26, 2011. http://simonmainwaring.com.

Facebook added a news feed feature that automatically let users know which friends had posted new information. Facebook was also used by organizations, which could create their own pages to keep their members informed and to publicize their activities.

A New Vulnerability

As increasing numbers of people (especially college and high school students) began to share the details of their lives online, this openness brought opportunity for self-expression and new relationships but also new kinds of vulnerability. Daniel J. Solove, an expert on the emerging issues of online law and issues of privacy and reputation, noted in 2008, "Openness is both good and bad. People can now spread their ideas everywhere without reliance on publishers, broadcasters or other traditional gatekeepers. But that transformation also creates profound threats to privacy and reputations."[38]

For young people social networks opened the way to cyberbullying, which could have tragic consequences. For example, in 2006 a teenager

A young man peruses his Facebook page. The 2004 launch of Facebook helped bring about a social networking revolution, opening up infinite possibilities for connecting with people around the world but also creating new opportunities for bullying and other harmful acts.

named Megan Taylor Meier hung herself three weeks before her fourteenth birthday. She had been first befriended, then bullied through the social network MySpace by "Josh Evans," a supposed sixteen-year-old boy who was actually the mother of a friend. One message from "Josh" read: "Everybody in O'Fallon [school] knows who you are. You are a bad person and everybody hates you. Have a [expletive] rest of your life. The world would be a better place without you."[39] Attempts to prosecute the offender ultimately failed—it appeared there was no law that could be used effectively. Since then, a number of jurisdictions have passed anti-cyberbullying laws, such as Missouri's Megan's Law.

Two teachers who founded the organization Children Online to help protect young people from online abuses noted that many students using social networks felt they could safely post whatever they wanted without any consequences. "Couple this false sense of privacy with the feeling of anonymity and lack of social responsibility that often develops from using text-centered telecommunications, and we see that many students post embarrassing, humiliating, denigrating and hurtful content in both text, photos, and videos," said the teachers. "We need to teach them that NOTHING IS PRIVATE online, especially their social networks."

They also noted that students could be victims as well as perpetrators: "Our students, though very knowledgeable about using technology, are often naive and easily manipulated (though they would hate to think so)."[40]

As valid as such concerns might be, it seemed unlikely that discouraging kids from going online or subjecting them to heavy-handed monitoring would work. As one professor suggested, both teachers and students needed to find appropriate ways to use the technology:

These days I hear from students via not only Facebook, and of course e-mail, but also texting and instant messaging. Within the context of boundaries I choose to set (for example, I do not answer text messages in the late evening), I try to respond in kind if the students' inquiries are simple. And I ask to switch to telephone or a face-to-face meeting if their questions are more complex. All told, I consider these exchanges to be worthwhile. The array of contact points made possible by various technologies can be seen as annoying and intrusive or full of possibility.[41]

The Political Impact of the Web

Social networks were not the only new way in which the web was being used to share information in the 2000s. A growing number of online users were writing blogs—regularly posted writings that could span a variety of topics from the personal to the political. The political impact of blogs was soon felt in some of the world's most troubled places—such as Iran.

In the mid-2000s Iran was in growing turmoil. By the end of the decade, thousands of reformers had taken to the streets to protest what they considered to be a rigged election result. Dozens were killed and many more arrested. As the government controlled the traditional media, bloggers and Twitter users became alternative channels for spreading news of the growing protests. One blogger explained:

> I keep a weblog so that I can breath[e] in this suffocating air. . . .
> In a society where one is taken to history's abattoir [slaughterhouse] for the mere crime of thinking, I write so as not to be lost in my despair, so that I feel that I am somewhere where my calls for justice can be uttered. I write a weblog so that I can shout, cry and laugh, and do the things that they have taken away from me in Iran today.[42]

The Iranian government repeatedly shut down or censored the Internet, while its opponents used software to get around the virtual roadblocks. Ultimately, despite considerable international support for the reformers, the conservative ruling party prevailed.

Nevertheless, the ability of users to quickly create and spread their own content on the web through blogs and recorded podcasts had become an increasingly important political factor—not only in the world's conflict spots, but in American election campaigns. As two campaign journalists suggested following the 2008 presidential race between Barack Obama and John McCain:

> This election was the first in which all candidates—presidential and congressional—attempted to connect directly with American voters via online social networking sites like Facebook and MySpace. It has even been called the "Facebook election." It is no coincidence that one of Obama's key strategists was 24-year-

old Chris Hughes, a Facebook cofounder. It was Hughes who masterminded the Obama campaign's highly effective Web blitzkrieg—everything from social networking sites to podcasting and mobile messaging.[43]

Iranians rally in Tehran in support of their defeated presidential candidate in 2009. Reformers accused the government of rigging the election that led to the defeat. They made their case to the world through blogs, podcasts, and other online tools.

A Challenge to Journalism

As blogs and other online media grew, print media—especially newspapers—found it hard to remain profitable. (Classified ads, traditionally a major source of revenue, were badly eroded by the popular Craigslist website.) In 2007 veteran journalist Robert Kuttner noted: "By the usual indicators, daily newspapers are in a deepening downward spiral. The new year brought reports of more newsroom layoffs, dwindling print circulation, flat or declining ad sales, increasing defections of readers and advertisers to the Internet, and sullen investors." However, Kuttner also noted that newspapers were beginning to try to do something about their plight: "Newspapers are embracing the Web with the manic enthusiasm of a convert. The Internet revenue of newspaper Web sites is increasing at 20 percent to 30 percent a year, and publishers are doing everything they can to boost Web traffic. Publishers know they are in a race against time, they are suddenly doing many things that their Internet competitors do, and often better."[44]

By the end of the decade, newspapers and magazines increasingly became available on e-reader devices such as Amazon's Kindle (introduced in 2007). Many print journalists began to offer blogs and maintain Facebook pages. Traditional journalism was beginning to be blended with the immediacy and personal dimension of blogging. As noted journalist-turned-blogger Andrew Sullivan writes:

> On my blog, my readers and I experienced 9/11 together, in real time. . . . There is a vividness to this immediacy that cannot be rivaled by print. The same goes for the 2000 [presidential election] recount, the Iraq War, the revelations of [prisoner abuse at] Abu Ghraib, the death of John Paul II, or any of the other history-making events of the past decade. . . . And the intimate bond this creates with readers is unlike the bond that the *Times*, say, develops with its readers through the same events.[45]

Wikis: Sharing Knowledge

The social face of the new web also expressed itself in new forms of cooperation. The ease with which people could find and make connections as well as post writings and images online meant that the whole really could be greater than the sum of its parts. Increasingly, people did not just read or view content—they created it. Content creation could be as simple as posting photos on sites such as Flickr or using the built-in capabilities of smartphones to post videos of everything from their cat falling into a fish tank to more serious images of riots, revolutions, or natural disasters.

People with a commitment to more sustained effort could write or revise articles for *Wikipedia*. Launched in January 2001 by Internet entrepreneur Jimmy Wales, this huge online encyclopedia grew out of the development in the 1990s by Ward Cunningham of WikiWikiWeb—a way to quickly and easily add, edit, or link texts using an ordinary web browser. (*Wiki* is a Hawaiian word meaning "fast" or "quick.") By March 2006 *Wikipedia* had added its one millionth article in English and was rapidly developing offshoots in other languages.

Anyone with minimal computer skills can contribute to *Wikipedia*, but the encyclopedia has mechanisms by which volunteers can review and edit articles. There are also special flags to keep track of material that might be controversial or subject to rapid change. (Statements not supported by citations are also noted.) This process of continual feedback and correction has usually worked well. A 2005 study published in *Nature* had experts compare *Wikipedia* articles with ones from the venerable *Encyclopaedia Britannica*. Both reference sources turned out to be mostly accurate, though *Wikipedia* had about a third more inaccuracies or omissions. Looking back in 2011, Jimmy Wales suggested:

> [For] people today who are coming up in the next generation, *Wikipedia* is going to be something that is always there and is the default standard way we go to get information. That means that we have an enormous responsibility at *Wikipedia* within our community to be open, to be transparent, to be accountable, and above all, to be very high quality, to be as good as we possibly can be.[46]

The Power and Vulnerability of Networks

The 2000s also saw a number of other cooperative projects where web users put their computers together to pursue a goal. For example, throughout the decade about 5 million people participated in a project involving the search for intelligent life on other worlds (Search for Extra-Terrestrial Intelligence, or SETI). The program, called SETI@home, installed software that ran in the background without disrupting normal computer use. The software automatically downloads and analyzes packets of data from the radio telescope at Arecibo in Puerto Rico, searching for signals that might indicate the presence of an alien intelligence. In essence, by working together the users created one of the world's most powerful supercomputer.

The ability to link computers and their users together thus offered ways to pool the efforts of potentially millions of people. But the same easy connectivity also appealed to those who wanted to use the networks for criminal purposes. Malicious hackers were harnessing the connectivity of the web, exploiting flaws in web browsers and operating systems or tricking users so that thousands of computers were enlisted in botnets. These hidden networks of compromised computers could be ordered to carry out commands without the knowledge of their users.

One of the most sophisticated botnets of the decade was called Conficker. First detected in November 2008, the self-reproducing computer worm used a variety of techniques to crack users' passwords and load itself onto vulnerable computers, repeating the process until millions of computers were enlisted. The processing power of the infected computers could then be sold to people who wanted to use them by remote control to send spam e-mail, attack websites, or steal information. With new capabilities come new vulnerabilities—an enduring theme for the new technology of the 2000s.

Chapter FIVE

The Human Past and Future

The science and technology of the 2000s not only brought new discoveries and inventions. A number of developments influenced how people viewed the origin and future of humanity itself. Fossils revealed new complexity in the story of how humans evolved over millions of years. Some intriguing possibilities about the relation of modern humans to ancestors such as the Neanderthals were revealed by genetic studies.

The increasingly rapid development of robotics challenged humanity in a different way. New robots that emerged during the decade were certainly not going to take over the world in science-fiction-movie fashion. Nevertheless, as robots started to appear in daily life, they began to change how people related to technology and perhaps began to blur the line between humans and intelligent machines.

Scientists also increasingly sounded an alarm about a threat to humanity's ability to continue to flourish on Earth. As evidence of global climate change continued to pile up, politicians struggled with difficult choices. At the same time some new technologies offered hope.

An Island in Time

In 2003 archaeologist Mike Morwood and his team were exploring the island of Flores in Indonesia. Inside a cave, they found a nearly complete skeleton of a hominin (human ancestor). Exploring further, the team found seven additional skeletons, dating from about thirty-eight thousand to thirteen thousand years ago. Any find of an early human is noteworthy, but there was something immediately striking about these creatures. They were only about 3 feet (1 m) tall. Their brains must have been much smaller than that of most hominin species, and their feet were unusually large. The species, given the scientific name *Homo floresiensis*, was soon dubbed "hobbits."

When the new species was declared in 2004, it aroused considerable skepticism in the scientific community. How could creatures with brains little larger than those of chimps have made the sophisticated stone tools found next to their remains or have used fire for cooking? Some critics suggested that these specimens did not represent a new species at all. Rather, critics argued, they were early modern humans who had suffered from a pathological condition called microcephaly that results in much smaller brains than normal. However, a 2007 analysis by anthropologist Dean Falk and her colleagues found that the "hobbit" skulls, while small, were similar in shape and structure to those of modern humans, with certain differences that were consistent with their being a separate species. Additionally, they found no sign of disease. But they did note that two parts of the hobbit brain, the frontal and temporal lobes, had developed differently from that of modern humans. This suggests that evolution may have found more than one way to develop a brain for a human tool user.

Scientists were also able to address the question of the species' small stature. Biologists have long observed that when a population of an animal is limited to an island like Flores, the food supply is limited. Smaller animals need less food and are thus more likely to survive and reproduce. They may also find it easier to regulate their body temperature. Paleoanthropologist Tim White observed that on Flores, "hominids are following the same evolutionary and ecological rules as other mammals. Darwin would have been delighted."[47]

A New Picture of Human Evolution

One of the enduring questions in paleoanthropology is when and how human ancestors became bipedal—that is, walked upright on two legs. During the 2000s several discoveries suggested that this important development in human evolution may have occurred much earlier than previously thought.

In 2001–2002 French paleoanthropologist Michel Brunet and his team discovered parts of a skull, jaws, and teeth of a species called *Sahelanthropus tchadensis*. Because such fossils are so fragile, it was not pos-

The small skull of a newly discovered species called Homo floresiensis *(left), is displayed in 2004 next to a modern human skull (right). The new species suggests that human evolution might have found more than one way to develop a brain for a human tool user.*

sible to open the skull to measure the size of the creature's brain. Instead, Brunet took the skull to a hospital and used a CT scanner. Using detailed images from the scan, Brunet was able to construct a 3-D virtual model of the skull. From this model he was able to precisely measure every dimension of the brain that had once been housed in that skull. Brunet determined something else as well. By measuring the angle at which the spinal cord was connected to the brain, Brunet concluded that this creature probably walked upright on two feet—it was bipedal.

Many scientists had thought that hominins became bipedal relatively late in their evolution, perhaps in response to the shrinking of the forest and the need to find food on the open grassy plains. The new evidence, however, suggests that hominins began to walk on two feet much earlier,

Should Nuclear Power Be Phased Out?

It might seem odd to use *nuclear* and *green* in the same sentence. However, the task of weaning the industrial and rapidly industrializing world off fossil fuels like coal, oil, and natural gas is a daunting one. Ultimately, many people favor clean, renewable forms of energy such as solar and wind. Even with their expansion during the 2000s, however, these forms of renewable energy could provide only a small percentage of the electricity generation needed.

Nuclear plants do not emit carbon dioxide or other greenhouse gases that contribute to warming. They do have accidents, however, some of which can be quite serious. They also produce tons of highly radioactive waste, and by the end of the 2000s decade the plan to store that waste in a huge repository inside Yucca Mountain, Nevada, had ground to a halt amid continuing safety and environmental concerns and opposition from local politicians.

Nevertheless, support for continuing nuclear power came from an unlikely source. In a 2005 magazine article, James Lovelock, famed for the idea of Earth as Gaia, a kind of super-organism, argued, "The benefits of using nuclear energy instead of fossil fuels are overwhelming. We know nuclear energy is safe, clean and effective because right now, 137 nuclear reactors are generating more than one-third of Western Europe's electricity and 440 in all are supplying one-seventh of the world's. . . . To phase out nuclear energy just when we need it most to combat global warming is madness."

James Lovelock, "Our Nuclear Lifeline," *Readers Digest*, March 2005. www.ecolo.org.

not long after human ancestors parted company with the ancestor of today's chimpanzees.

A discovery announced in October 2009 provided further evidence for the view that human ancestors began walking on two legs more than 4 million years ago. That discovery also revealed which other creatures shared the world with the earliest human ancestors. Fossils from a group of more than thirty-five of the 4.4-million-year-old hominins named *Ardipithecus ramidus* ("Ardi" for short) were found buried in volcanic ash in the Middle Awash, an area in Ethiopia famous for fossil finds.

Besides adding to the evidence for bipedalism, the Ethiopian find also provided important details about how these early human ancestors lived. Prominent University of California–Berkeley paleoanthropologist Tim White noted that thousands of other animal fossils were also found in the area: "This gave us a series of fantastic, high-resolution snapshots across an ancient landscape—a true picture of what Ardi's habitat was like. It tells us that long before hominids developed tools or big brains or ranged the open savanna, they were walking upright."[48]

The decade also yielded powerful new tools in a field where drawings and photographs had been the main way to depict fossils. Science writer Carl Zimmer notes that computed tomography (CT) scans and modern computer animation are being used to learn about intriguing aspects of early humans and to make precious fossils more accessible to researchers:

> As the use of CT scans expands, paleoanthropologists are developing new avenues for uncovering clues to our past. They are discovering signs of healed wounds, of toothless old hominids who must have been cared for by others. Some researchers are even producing full-length virtual skeletons to which they can attach virtual muscles and make the ancient hominids walk again. Most significantly, CT scans can liberate hominid fossils from museum drawers. Once a research team makes a scan, they can post the data on a Web site for other researchers to analyze, bringing a precious hominid fossil to new sets of eyes and new sets of questions.[49]

Neanderthals: Closer than Cousins?

Ever since the first fossils were discovered in the mid-nineteenth century, Neanderthals have fascinated both scientists and the general public. Both the origin and extinction of the species remain in dispute. Hominins with Neanderthal characteristics may have lived in Europe as long as six hundred thousand years ago. Neanderthals disappear from the fossil record somewhere between twenty-five thousand and thirty-five thousand years ago.

Despite their caricature in cartoons as brutish, club-wielding cave dwellers, Neanderthals actually had larger brains than modern humans. They made a variety of tools, used fire, and lived in small groups. They also seem to have built shelters out of animal bones. They may have made jewelry and painted pictures in caves. One problem with determining the extent of Neanderthal culture is that Neanderthals and early modern humans (sometimes called Cro-Magnons) lived in the same areas, so it is often not clear which type of human produced a given artifact.

One of the most intriguing and controversial questions is whether Neanderthals used language beyond grunts and hand signals. By the 2000s researchers had a new tool that might help answer this question: DNA analysis. By 2003 the genome of modern humans had been spelled out. In 2009 evolutionary biologist Svante Pääbo and colleagues sequenced a portion of the Neanderthal genome. They found that Neanderthals had the mutations in a gene that is associated with language in humans. Pääbo concluded, "From the data we have so far, there is no reason to assume that Neanderthals could not speak like we do." He adds that ongoing research will help pinpoint "those few genetic changes that are crucial for modern human behavior and ability."[50]

Intriguing Possibilities

For at least several thousand years (maybe more), Neanderthals and modern humans shared many areas of Europe. The question of why the Neanderthals died out remains. Various theories, including the inability to adapt to the warming climate between ice ages and decimation from diseases carried by invaders, have been suggested.

There is another possibility. The Neanderthals did not disappear; rather, they became part of modern humanity. That is, some Neanderthals may have bred with modern humans. Erik Trinkaus, a prominent expert on Neanderthals, claimed in a 2006 book that certain fossils represented hybrid combinations of Neanderthal and modern human characteristics. But interpretation of fossils is notoriously difficult and prone to dispute. What do the genes have to say?

In May 2010 Pääbo and his group at Germany's Max Planck Institute published a draft of the complete Neanderthal genome. They found that while modern humans trace their ancestry to Africa, between 1 and 4 percent of the human genome may have come from Neanderthals. "They are not totally extinct. In some of us they live on, a bit,"[51] remarked Pääbo.

The Rise of the Robots

On New Year's Eve in 2001, the Japanese pop group Snap was performing a dance on live TV. One of the performers, only 4 feet (1.2 m) tall, was a robot called Asimo. Unlike the hulking, clunky, often dangerous robots of bad science-fiction movies, Asimo moved fluidly. Teams of researchers around the world had worked for decades to make robots that could walk rather than roll. (Walking makes it easier to get around obstacles, not to

The robot Asimo demonstrates its ability to kick a soccer ball. The development of robot technology during the 2000s suggested new possibilities for the use of robots in the future.

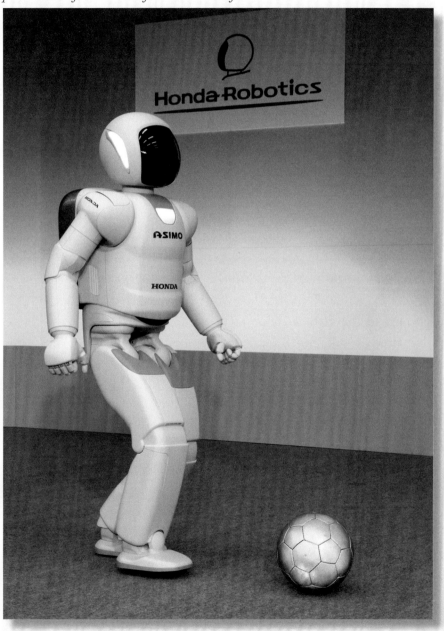

mention going up and down stairs.) Walking, something most people have done without thinking since they were toddlers, involves a complex flow of muscles, reflexes, and balance. But here was a robot that could keep up with a fast dance number. Asimo, built by the Honda Corporation, tracked its shifting center of gravity and knew how to turn, twist, or change from a walk to a run. Soon, Asimo robots, with their ability to maneuver easily as they interacted with people, were being rented by corporations to serve as receptionists or guides.

Other robots that began to be used more widely in the 2000s did not look like small people but more like mobile copy machines. A robot called HelpMate (designed in the late 1990s) began roaming hospital corridors to deliver drugs and supplies. What is special about this robot is its sophisticated vision system that enables it to recognize different types of obstacles at different distances and maneuver to avoid them. The robot can even electronically summon an elevator and ride it to the needed floor. The robots are monitored by a wireless network. They can communicate with each other, but also with people they meet throughout the hospital. In 2004 Susan Dierker, a nursing supervisor, enthused, "They're wonderful and they talk to you in Spanish and English. The nursing staff is pleased with them and most people just stare because they're wandering around the hospital."[52]

Visions of the Future

The ultimate robot that futurists envisioned would have human-like intelligence and understanding and perform any household chore or personal service. Japan, with a growing population of elderly people, has also been particularly keen to develop robots. Ideally these robots would be able to assist older people, who often live alone, with their daily tasks and to detect when medical or other help might be needed. Numerous challenges would have to be met before such robots become reality.

Nevertheless, researchers in the 2000s took the first steps toward robots with this kind of versatility. By 2008 at Massachusetts Institute of Technology, the Nexi robot was being given a human-like head and the ability to convey expressions (such as raised eyebrows), while the self-balancing wheel body had a mechanism similar to that of a Segway scooter. Other aspects of the research involved the software, which enabled the

The Perils of Prediction

The science-fiction writers of the 1940s and 1950s wrote about the 2000s as a time when people would have established colonies on the moon and Mars. A bustling mining industry in the asteroid belt would offer plentiful opportunities. Space would be the place to act out the dreams of the human race.

By the real 2000s humans had last walked on the moon three decades earlier. The solar system was being explored by robots but not colonized by people. The real action was in cyberspace, not outer space. Virtually no one had predicted the personal computer, let alone the World Wide Web.

If people in the 1950s got the 2000s wrong, what did people in the 2000s think would be happening by the middle of the new century? In a 2005 book, inventor and futurist Ray Kurzweil gives predictions based on the ever-increasing power of computers and advances in nanotechnology and artificial intelligence. He predicted that tiny nanomachines would roam human bodies and even brains, repairing damage and enhancing thinking and memory. Mental problems could be fixed by rewiring the brain. The contents of whole human brains could be backed up to a computer server, which would benefit someone who suffered severe brain injury. Some people might choose to live in enhanced bodies that have what today would be called superpowers. Others might choose to live in cyberspace as pure thought.

Is Kurzweil right? Many people alive today may find out.

Ray Kurzweil, *The Singularity Is Near: When Humans Transcend Biology*. New York: Penguin, 2006.

robot to understand and better communicate and cooperate with human workers. After a video of Nexi was posted on YouTube in 2008, viewer comments ranged from awe and bemusement to shock and alarm.

Finally, there was a robot that people could actually buy and take home to do useful work. Introduced in 2002, the little disc-shaped vacuum cleaner called Roomba is 13 inches (33 cm) in diameter and less than 3.5 inches (9 cm) in height. It is far from the smartest robot ever built, but it has a few clever features. It is programmed to follow a random but generally spiral path around a room. When it bumps into something, it reverses itself. If it detects a wall, it follows it so a special brush can collect the dirt from edges and corners. It can also tell how dirty a particular area is and spend more time making sure that area is cleaned. Roomba was soon followed by Scooba, a robot that could mop the floor.

By the end of the decade, about 5 million Roombas had been sold at about $200 each. Colin Angle, whose company iRobot developed the machine, told an interviewer what he thought was the deeper significance of getting this little robot into millions of ordinary households: "The Roomba is a first step. It's not intimidating. And it works. People find that surprising. The Roomba has gotten more people to accept the idea that robots can be useful. . . . Then think about robots taking care of people, especially for elder care. That will be the killer application for robotics."[53]

A Warming Planet

The first decade of the twenty-first century turned out to be the hottest ever recorded. Scientists know this because of what they have learned from deep-ice cores and fossils about average annual temperatures going back thousands of years. With solar cycles, levels of volcanic activity, and other natural processes that can also cause warming accounted for, by the end of the 2000s it became clear that human industrial activity since the eighteenth century was a major culprit in a warming Earth. The cause was the growing concentration of carbon dioxide, methane, and other gases produced mainly by burning coal and other fossil fuels. These greenhouse gases trap heat from the sun and prevent it from being radiated away into space.

An extensive and thoroughly documented study by the United Nations Intergovernmental Panel on Climate Change (IPCC), conducted from 2002 to 2007, confirmed the growing body of evidence. The Earth was running a fever, and the symptoms were likely to get worse. Former vice president Al Gore's book and film *An Inconvenient Truth* helped publicize the gravity of the situation, and in 2007 Gore and the IPCC jointly received the Nobel Peace Prize for their efforts.

The effect on the climate is not a simple, uniform warming of the whole planet. The effects vary in different places. In 2002, for example, Larson B, a huge ice shelf in Antarctica that had been firmly attached to the coast for thousands of years, broke up. A heat wave gripped Europe in the summer of 2003 and is estimated to have killed about thirty thousand people—mostly the elderly, the sick, and those with inadequate cooling. Another even more dramatic and deadly phenomenon is fueled by the extra heat energy being stored in the ocean—hurricanes. In 2005 scientists looking at records concluded that there were then, on average, twice as many Category 4 and 5 hurricanes—the most destructive kind. One of them, Hurricane Katrina, killed more than eighteen hundred people, mostly from flooding around New Orleans, in 2005. Meanwhile, polar bears were dying in the Arctic because they could not find ice floes to camp on. However, the vanishing of Arctic ice was also beginning to open a passage that ships might use to get from the Atlantic to the Pacific.

A Slow Response
Response of world leaders to the complex issues raised by climate change was rather slow. In 1997 the United Nations agreement called the Kyoto

Water pours down the face of a melting glacier in Norway. Studies conducted by scientists in the 2000s brought warnings of global warming resulting from increases in greenhouse gas emissions.

Protocol was adopted. Its intention was to reduce global greenhouse gas emissions—a modest decrease of about 10 percent compared to 1990 levels. President Bill Clinton signed for the United States, but in 2001 the new president, George W. Bush, withdrew from the agreement, citing potential harm to the American economy.

Critics of the Kyoto Protocol considered it to be too little, too late. The huge developing industrial nations of China, India, and Brazil were not required to reduce their carbon emissions. Meanwhile, throughout the 2000 decade the United States continued to produce about 25 percent of global greenhouse gas emissions.

In December 2009 a new climate change summit was held in Copenhagen, Denmark. Participants hoped that, at last, they could agree on substantial, firm emission-reduction targets that could actually have an effect on climate change. Plagued by disagreements, the talks broke down. President Barack Obama then negotiated a separate accord with China, India, South Africa, and Brazil. It set a goal of limiting the global temperature rise to 3.6°F (2°C) above preindustrial levels by 2050. The nations also agreed to monitor their progress, but again, it looked to critics that the commitments were not serious or definite enough. The challenge was passed to a new decade.

The Greening of Technology

A crowd watches a thrilling automobile race. The winner, a sleek rocket-shaped vehicle, is an electric car. Clean, smooth-running electric cars are easy to start, drive, and stop. Surely they are the wave of the future. So might the audience at the racetrack have felt on April 29, 1899. For the first two decades or so of the twentieth century, electric cars competed quite successfully with those powered by gasoline-fueled internal combustion engines. However, the bulky batteries and short range of electric vehicles proved to be no match for the energy packed into cheap gasoline.

By the 1990s, battery technology, while still one of the biggest challenges to electric car designers, had begun to improve. During the 2000 decade sales of hybrid vehicles began to take off, aided by the introduction of lithium-ion (l-ion) batteries. Hybrid cars can use electricity for short-range trips and switch to gasoline for longer ranges or when maximum power is needed. Hybrids feature smooth acceleration and the ability to manage energy quite efficiently, such as by recapturing energy generated by braking. This efficiency is aided by the growing use of computer technology for virtually every system in the vehicle. The Toyota Prius, introduced worldwide in 2000, proved to be the most popular hybrid of the decade. In 2008 Tesla Motors introduced its Roadster, an all-electric sports car that can hit 125 miles per hour (201 kph). While the $100,000 vehicle was hardly suitable for the majority of car buyers, the publicity raised interest in more practical and affordable electric vehicles such as the Chevy Volt and Nissan Leaf, which hit the market at the beginning of the next decade.

Hybrid cars have reduced greenhouse emissions, but the electricity they and their pure electric cousins use has to be generated somehow. The other parts of the climate challenge thus involve reducing overall use of electricity and generating power from renewable, nonpolluting sources such as solar and wind power. During the 2000s solar power, particularly photovoltaic cells, grew in popularity and efficiency while becoming cheaper. In many applications (including buildings), the older sheet form of solar cells began to be replaced by thin film solar cells. As one writer notes: "Because thin-film panels are both lightweight and flexible, it's possible to incorporate them directly into buildings—as roofing materials, for example." The same writer noted that these versatile solar power cells are rapidly finding new applications in awnings, facades, and even windows. "For every new technological development that's announced, there are dozens more in the works. Future generations will wonder why people ever used fossil fuels to produce electricity.[54]

Will human ingenuity and resourcefulness catch up with climate change? It will take another decade or two to find out. But during the 2000s scientists, engineers, and entrepreneurs showed their imagination and resourcefulness in new discoveries and technologies. Perhaps that ingenuity only needs to be matched by the willingness of people to make better choices about how they use technology—and how they obtain the energy they need.

Chapter One: Cellular Secrets

1. Quoted in Kathleen McCauliffe, "First Synthetic Organism Created," *Discover*, January/February 2011. http://discovermagazine.com.

2. Quoted in Sheryl Gay Stolberg, "The Biotech Death of Jesse Gelsinger," *New York Times*, November 28, 1999. www.nytimes.com.

3. Quoted in Jocelyn Kaiser, "Gene Therapy in a New Light," *Smithsonian*, January 2009, pp. 54-61.

4. Pam Belluck, "Giving Sight by Therapy with Genes," *New York Times*, November 2, 2009. www.nytimes.com.

5. Quoted in Belluck, "Giving Sight by Therapy with Genes."

6. Quoted in Cedars-Sinai, "First Human Receives Cardiac Stem Cells in Clinical Trial to Heal Damage Caused by Heart Attacks," news release, June 30, 2009. www.cedars-sinai.edu.

7. Quoted in J.L., "Can You Buy a Cure in China?," *Discover*, November 2009, p. 35.

8. Quoted in Nicole Dyer, "A Toast to the Bionic Man," *Popular Science*, September 19, 2005. www.popsci.com.

9. Quoted in Susan Kruglinksi, "The Blue Brain Project," *Discover*, December 2007, p. 50-52.

10. Quoted in Kruglinski, "The Blue Brain Project."

Chapter Two: Exploring the Cosmos

11. Quoted in Mars Exploration Rovers, "Girl with Dream Names Mars Rovers *Spirit* and *Opportunity*," press release, June 08, 2003. www.nasa.gov.

12. Quoted in Elizabeth Rusch, *The Mighty Mars Rovers: The Incredible Adventures of* Spirit *and* Opportunity. Boston: Houghton Mifflin, 2012, p. 26.

13. Quoted in Rusch, *The Mighty Mars Rovers*, p. 26.

14. Quoted in Mark Hachman, "DOS Glitch Nearly Killed Mars Rover," *PC Magazine*, August 23, 2004. www.pcmag.com.

15. Quoted in Adam Fisher, "Very Stunning, Very Space, and Very Cool: The Launch of Space Tourism," *Technology Review*, January/February 2009, p. 64.

16. Quoted in Michael D. Lemonick, *Mirror Earth: The Search for Our Planet's Twin.* New York: Walker, 2012, p. 163.

17. Ray Jayawardhana. *Strange New Worlds: The Search for Alien Planets and Life Beyond Our Solar System.* Princeton, NJ: Princeton University Press, 2011, p. 149.

18. Quoted in Jeanna Bryner, "First-Ever Images Taken of Extrasolar Planets," NBCNews.com, November 13, 2008. www.nbcnews.com.

Chapter Three: Mysteries of Energy and Matter

19. Quoted in Gabrielle Walker, "The Biggest Thing in Physics," *Discover*, August 2007. http://discovermagazine.com.

20. Quoted in Walker, "The Biggest Thing in Physics."

21. Quoted in Alex Stone, "Cosmic Collision Brings Dark Matter into View," *Discover*, January 2007, p. 25.

22. Quoted in Stone, "Cosmic Collision Brings Dark Matter into View." p. 25.

23. Quoted in NASA, "Astrophysicist Adam Riess Wins the 2011 Nobel Prize in Physics," news release, HubbleSite, October 4, 2011. http://hubblesite.org.

24. Quoted in NASA, "NASA's Hubble Finds Evidence for Dark Energy in the Young Universe," news release, November 16, 2006. www.nasa.gov.

25. Quoted in NASA, "Astrophysicist Adam Riess Wins the 2011 Nobel Prize in Physics."

26. NASA, "New Image of Infant Universe Reveals Era of First Stars, Age of Cosmos, and More," February 11, 2003. www.nasa.gov.

27. Quoted in NASA, "New Image of Infant Universe Reveals Era of First Stars, Age of Cosmos, and More."

28. Mihail C. Roco, "Nanotechnology's Future," *Scientific American*. July 24, 2006. www.scientificamerican.com.

29. Quoted in *The Daily Galaxy* (blog), "Is the Age of Silicon Computing Coming to an End?," May 1, 2012. www.dailygalaxy.com.

30. Quoted in *Yale News* (New Haven, CT), "Scientists Create First Electronic Quantum Processor," June 28, 2009. http://news.yale.edu.

31. Quoted in Stefan Lovgren, "Computer Made from DNA and Enzymes," *National Geographic*, February 24, 2003. http://news.nationalgeographic.com.

Chapter Four: Going Mobile and Getting Social

32. "Ranking Nodes in a Graph," Google Patent Filing US7076483 B2. www.google.com/patents/US7076483.

33. Harry McCracken, "iPhone Recap: PCW's Review, Videos, and More," *PC World*, June 30, 2007. http://web.archive.org.

34. Walter Isaacson, *Steve Jobs*. New York: Simon & Schuster, 2011.

35. John Cassidy, "Me Media: How Hanging Out on the Internet Became Big Business," *New Yorker*, May 15, 2006.www.newyorker.com.

36. Quoted in Alan Tabak, "Hundreds Register for New Facebook Website," *Harvard Crimson* (Harvard University, Cambridge, MA), February 9, 2004. www.thecrimson.com.

37. Quoted in Cassidy, "Me Media."

38. Daniel J. Solove, "Do Social Networks Bring the End of Privacy?," *Scientific American*, September 2008, p. 100–106.

39. Quoted in Kate E. Schwartz, "Criminal Liability for Internet Culprits: The Need for Updated State Laws Covering Full Spectrum of Cyber Victimization," *Washington University Law Review*, vol. 87, no. 2, 2010, p. 407.

40. Doug Fodeman and Marje Monroe, "The Impact of Facebook on Our Students," Children Online. www.childrenonline.org.

41. Quoted in Harriet L. Schwartz, "Facebook: The New Classroom Commons?," *Chronicle of Higher Education*, October 2, 2009 p. B12-B13.

42. Quoted in Bill Berkeley, "Bloggers vs. Mullahs: How the Internet Roils Iran," *World Policy Journal*, Spring 2006, p. 73.

43. Matthew Fraser and Soumitra Dutta, "Barack Obama and the Facebook Election," *U.S. News & World Report*, November 19, 2008. www.usnews.com.

44. Robert Kuttner, "The Race," *Columbia Journalism Review*, March 1, 2007. www.cjr.org.

45. Andrew Sullivan, "Why I Blog," *Atlantic*, November 2008. www.theatlantic.com.

46. Quoted in Josh Goldman, "Founder Explains Impact of *Wikipedia*," *Student Life* (Washington University, St. Louis), March 28, 2011. www.studlife.com.

Chapter Five: The Human Past and Future

47. Quoted in Michael W. Robbins, "Little People Make Big Splash," *Discover*, January 2005, p. 31.

48. Quoted in Jill Neimark, "Meet Your New Ancestor," *Discover*, January/February 2010, p. 22.

49. Carl Zimmer, "Human Origins: Commonplace Hospital Gear Opens Up a New Way of Reconstructing Forerunners of Homo Sapiens," *Discover*, October 2005, pp. 40–41

50. Quoted in Jill Neimark, "Neanderthals Get Personal," *Discover*, January 2010, p. 4.

51. Quoted in BBC News, "Neanderthal Genes 'Survive in Us,'" May 6, 2010. http://news.bbc.co.uk.

52. Quoted in Mike Crissey, "Courier Robots Get Traction in Hospitals After Fits and Starts," *USA Today*, July 6, 2004. http://usatoday30.usatoday.com.

53. Quoted in *BloombergBusinessweek*, "Robots: Today, Roomba. Tomorrow. . . ," May 5, 2004. www.businessweek.com.

54. Steve Heckeroth, "The Promise of Thin-Film Solar," *Mother Earth News*, February/March 2010. www.motherearthnews.com.

Jeff Bezos: The founder of Amazon, he turned an online bookstore into a huge business that sells just about everything that is legal.

Francis Collins: An American geneticist and physician who headed the federally sponsored Human Genome Project.

Kim Eric Drexler: An engineer, entrepreneur, and writer who popularized nanotechnology starting in the 1980s.

Al Gore: A former US vice president, Gore is an environmentalist and advocate for dealing with climate change.

Steve Jobs: The cofounder of Apple Computer (now deceased), Jobs returned to the company in the late 1990s and led it to develop the iPod, iPhone, and other mobile devices and media services.

Geoffrey Marcy: An American astronomer and pioneer in the discovery of extrasolar planets.

Svante Pääbo: A Swedish evolutionary biologist best known for his study of the genetics of the Neanderthals and other early humans.

Larry Page and Sergey Brin: The founders of Google, they developed a more effective search engine, advertising programs, mobile operating systems, and an expanding empire of media and services.

Burt Rutan: An aerospace engineer whose innovative designs include the *Voyager*, a world-circling airplane, and the private spacecraft, *SpaceShipOne*.

Steve Squyres: An astronomer and planetary scientist who led the science team for the Mars Exploration Rover program.

Sherry Turkle: A psychologist and social scientist who has extensively studied the effects of computer technology on users.

J. Craig Venter: A biologist and entrepreneur who led Celera Genomics and the private branch of the effort to sequence the human genome; he developed innovative methods for gene sequencing.

Jimmy Wales: The founder of *Wikipedia*, the world's most extensive on-line reference source.

Mark Zuckerberg: A Harvard student who turned a dorm project into Facebook, a social network with 1.1 billion users by 2013.

Note: Below is a sampling of new words or words given new meaning during the decade, taken from a variety of sources.

bailout: Rescue by government of companies on the brink of failure.

birther: A person who believes that Barack Obama was not born in the United States and therefore cannot be president.

bling: Ostentatious displays of fortune and flash.

blog: A weblog.

chad: The tiny paper square that pops out when a voter punches the ballot card while casting a vote.

Chinglish: The growing Chinese-English hybrid language resulting from China's expanding influence.

click-through: Clicking on a banner ad on a website.

cloud computing: The practice of storing regularly used computer data on multiple servers that can be accessed through the Internet.

distracted driving: Multitasking while driving.

frenemy: Someone who is both friend and enemy.

generica: Strip malls, motel chains, prefab housing, and other features of the American landscape that are the same nationwide.

hacktivism: Activism by hackers.

hashtag: The # (hash) symbol used as a tag on Twitter.

helicopter mom/dad: A parent who micromanages his or her children's lives and is perceived to be hovering over every stage of their development.

locavore: Someone who cooks and eats locally grown food.

meh: Boring, apathetic, or unimpressive.

plutoed: To be demoted or devalued, as happened to the former planet Pluto.

push present: An expensive gift given to a woman by her husband in appreciation for having recently given birth.

red state/blue state: States whose residents predominantly vote Republican (red states) or Democrat (blue states).

same-sex marriage: Marriage of gay couples.

sandwich generation: People in their forties or fifties who are caring for young children and elderly parents at the same time.

sexting: Sending of sexually explicit text messages and pictures via cell phones.

snollygoster: A shrewd, unprincipled person; often used to refer to a politician.

staycation: A holiday spent at home and involving day trips to local attractions.

truthiness: Something one wishes to be the truth regardless of the facts.

tweet: To send a message via Twitter.

twixters: Adult men and women who still live with their parents.

unfriend: To remove someone from a friends list on a social networking site such as Facebook.

zombie bank: A financial institution kept alive only through government funding.

Books

Earl Boysen and Nancy Boysen, *Nanotechnology for Dummies*. 2nd ed. Hoboken, NJ: Wiley, 2011.

Rodney Brooks, *Flesh and Machines: How Robots Will Change Us*. New York: Pantheon, 2002.

Ann Gibbons, *The First Human: The Race to Discover Our Earliest Ancestors*. New York: Anchor, 2007.

Ray Jayawardhana, *Strange New Worlds: The Search for Alien Planets and Life Beyond Our Solar System*. Princeton, NJ: Princeton University Press, 2011.

Ray Kurzweil, *The Singularity Is Near: When Humans Transcend Biology*. New York: Penguin, 2006.

Michael D. Lemonick, *Mirror Earth: The Search for Our Planet's Twin*. New York: Walker, 2012.

Ricki Lewis, *The Forever Fix: Gene Therapy and the Boy Who Saved It*. New York: St. Martin's Griffin, 2013.

Noel Merino, ed., *Human Genetics*. Farmington Hills, MI: Greenhaven, 2010.

Iain Nicholson, *Dark Side of the Universe: Dark Matter, Dark Energy, and the Fate of the Cosmos*. Baltimore: Johns Hopkins University Press, 2007.

Richard Panek, *The 4 Percent Universe: Dark Matter, Dark Energy, and the Race to Discover the Rest of Reality*. Boston: Houghton Mifflin, 2011.

Eric Schmidt and Jared Cohen, *The New Digital Age: Reshaping the Future of People, Nations, and Business*. New York: Knopf, 2013.

Gavin Schmidt and Joshua Wolfe, *Climate Change: Picturing the Science*. New York: Norton, 2009.

Jonathan Slack, *Stem Cells: A Very Short Introduction*. New York: Oxford University Press, 2012.

Steve Squyres, *Roving Mars: Spirit, Opportunity, and the Exploration of the Red Planet*. New York: Hyperion, 2006.

Roger Wiens, *Red Rover: Inside the Story of Robotic Space Exploration, from Genesis to the Mars Rover* Curiosity. Philadelphia: Basic Books, 2013.

Websites

Discovery News (http://news.discovery.com). Organizes news about science, technology, and adventure travel by topic. Sample tags: evolution, genetics, biotechnology, and robotics.

Extrasolar Planet News (www.sciencedaily.com/news/space_time/extrasolar_planets). Extensive news of discoveries and mission progress. Part of *ScienceDaily*, which covers many other science topics as well.

Genetics Education Center, University of Kansas Medical Center (www.kumc.edu/gec). Extensive links to background and discussions, including material from the National Human Genome Research Institute, resources for students and teachers, and career links.

Internet World Stats (www.internetworldstats.com). Provides up-to-date statistics on Internet usage, e-commerce, market research, and other resources, organized by region and country.

Large Hadron Collider (http://home.web.cern.ch/about/accelerators/large-hadron-collider). News (and everything else) about the world's largest scientific research facility.

National Nanotechnology Initiative (www.nano.gov). Represents nanotechnology-related activities of twenty-seven US federal agencies. Includes background resources and news.

Pew Internet & American Life Project (www.pewinternet.org). Offers extensive and frequently updated research studies about how the Internet is used and the issues it raises.

Social Networking Watch (www.socialnetworkingwatch.com). Includes latest news and statistics about social networks such as Facebook, LinkedIn, and Google+.

Spirit and Opportunity: Mars Exploration Rovers (www.nasa.gov /mission_pages/mer/index.html). Latest news, images, and detailed information about the two Mars rovers, as well as related and future NASA missions.

Stem Cell Resources (www.stemcellresources.org). Provides news and resources for teachers and students interested in stem cell research, including links to animations and other media.

Index

Note: Boldface page numbers indicate illustrations.

Foundation Fighting Blindness, 15

Freedom space station proposal, 39

Gaia concept, 66

galaxy collisions, 38–41, **40**

Galileo (Jupiter probe), 23

Gelsinger, Jesse, 12

gene therapy, 12–15, 43

genes, 11, 14, 47–48

genetic tests, 18

glaciers, **73**

God particle, search for, 10

Google, 8, 49–50, 52

Gore, Al, 72

Greely, Hank, 18

greenhouse gas emissions, 74, 75

Haas, Corey, 15

hackers, 62

Hearst, William Randolph, 31

HelpMate, 70

Higgs boson, 10, 36

"hobbits," 63–64, **65**

Homo floresiensis, 63–64, **65**

Honda Corporation, 70

hot dark matter, 38–39

Hubble Space Telescope, 27, 34

Hughes, Chris, 59

human evolution

  bipedalism, 64–66

  Homo floresiensis, 63–64, **65**

  Neanderthals, 67–68

Human Genome Project, **13**

  accomplishments of, 11

  completion of, 10

  Neanderthal genome, 68

  percent human of genes from Neanderthals, 68

humans, designing, 14

hurricanes, 73

Huygens mission, 23–24

hybrid cars, 74–75

IBM Blue Gene (supercomputer), 22

IBM Roadrunner (supercomputer), 46

ice shelves, 72, **73**

Inconvenient Truth, An (Gore: book and film), 72

Indonesia, 63–64

Intergovernmental Panel on Climate Change (IPCC), 72

International Space Station, 27, 30–31, 32, 39

Io (moon of Jupiter), 23

iPhones, 9, 50, **51**, 52

iPods, 9, 50–52

Iran, 58, **59**

Isaacson, Walter, 50

iTunes Store, 51–52

Japan, 68–70, **69**

Jayawardhana, Ray, 34

Jobs, Steve, 8, 50

journalism, 60

Joy, Bill, 43

Jupiter probe, 23

Kaku, Michio, 46

Krauss, Lawrence M., 27

Kurzweil, Ray, 43, 71

Kuttner, Robert, 60

Kyoto Protocol (1997), 73–74

Kyoto University, 17

Lagrange 2 location, 42

Large Hadron Collider (LHC), 10, 35–39, **37**

Harry Henderson has written more than thirty books on science and technology, particularly computing, including technical, historical, and biographical works. He lives with his wife, Lisa Yount (a retired writer and active artist), in El Cerrito, California.